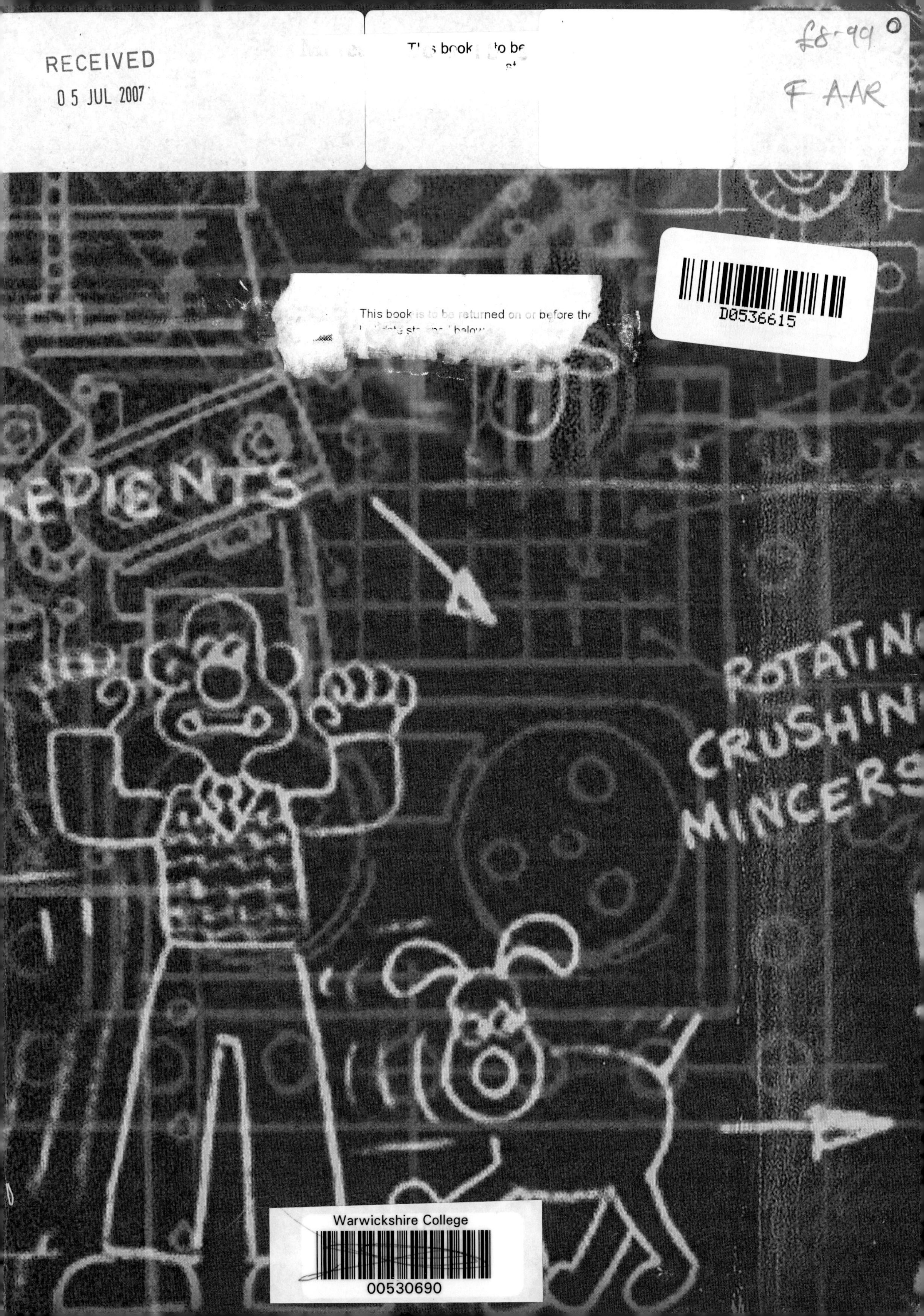
ROTATIN
CRUSHIN
MINCERS

Aardman
presents

Wallace & Gromit ™

Catch of
the Day

Titan Books

Wallace & Gromit
Catch of the Day

HB ISBN 1 84023 495 4
PB ISBN 1 84023 496 2

Published by Titan Books,
a division of Titan Publishing Group Ltd.
144 Southwark St
London SE1 0UP
In association with Aardman Animation Ltd.

Grateful thanks and salutations to
Dick Hansom and Rachael Carpenter at Aardman Animation,
David Barraclough, Bob Kelly, Adam Newell, Angie Thomas
and Jamie Boardman at Titan Books, and Bambos Georgiou.

A CIP catalogue record for this title is available from the British Library.

First edition: November 2002
2 4 6 8 10 9 7 5 3

Printed in Italy.

What did you think of this book? We love
to hear from our readers. Please email us
at: readerfeedback@titanemail.com, or
write to us at the above address.

Aardman

presents

Wallace & Gromit™
Catch of
the Day

Original story by Simon Furman and Katy Wild

Written by Ian Rimmer

Drawn by Jimmy Hansen

Coloured by John Burns

Lettered by Richard Starkings
and Comicraft's Saida!

Designed by Caroline Grimshaw

Edited by Simon Furman

Wallace and Gromit created by Nick Park

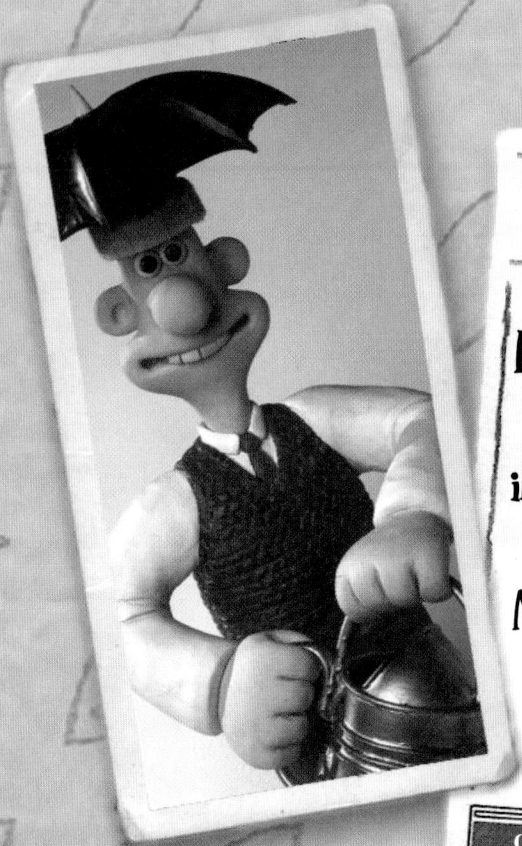

WALLACE

No. 1

Part-time handyman, enthusiastic inventor and cheese connoisseur.
No job too big, no solution too straightforward.

Issued by
CRACKING CONFECTIONERY
LONDON - - - ENGLAND
PRINTED IN ENGLAND

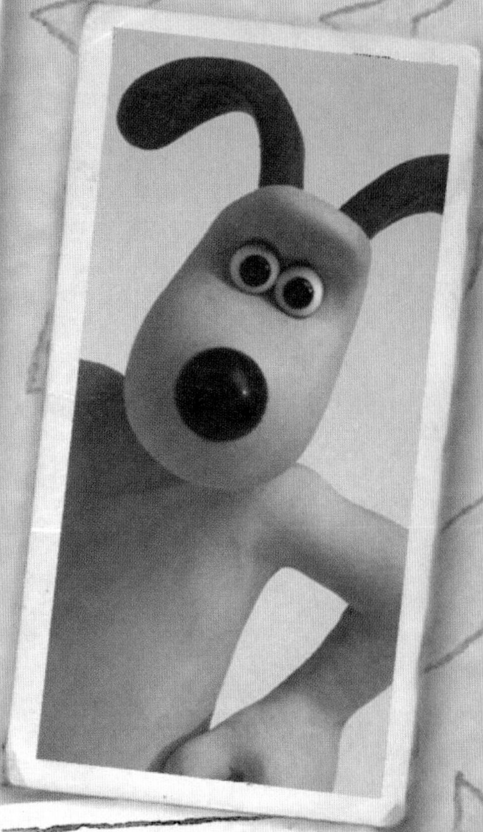

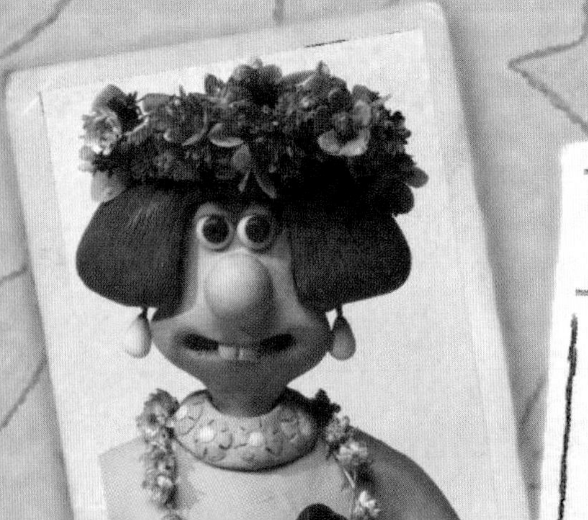

WENDOLENE

No. 3

Owner of the town's Wool Shop and object of Wallace's unspoken affections. Tea and sympathy a specialty.

Issued by
CRACKING CONFECTIONERY
LONDON - - - ENGLAND
PRINTED IN ENGLAND

GROMIT

No. 2

Long-suffering but faithful companion, sidekick and occasional dogsbody. Yearns for the quiet life, doesn't get it.

Issued by
CRACKING CONFECTIONERY
LONDON - - - ENGLAND
PRINTED IN ENGLAND

SHAUN

No. 4

Lost sheep and all-round appetite on legs. Eats anything, anywhere. Fleeced but not stirred.

Issued by
CRACKING CONFECTIONERY
LONDON - - - ENGLAND
PRINTED IN ENGLAND

PRESTON

No. 5

Wayward robotic pooch and former sheep-rustler. Got pressed in his own machinery and re-packaged.

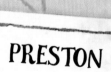

Issued by
CRACKING CONFECTIONERY
LONDON - - - ENGLAND
PRINTED IN ENGLAND

FEATHERS McGRAW

No. 6

Notorious criminal mastermind and bird of many faces. Got caught with his pants down and put on ice.

Issued by
CRACKING CONFECTIONERY
LONDON - - - ENGLAND
PRINTED IN ENGLAND

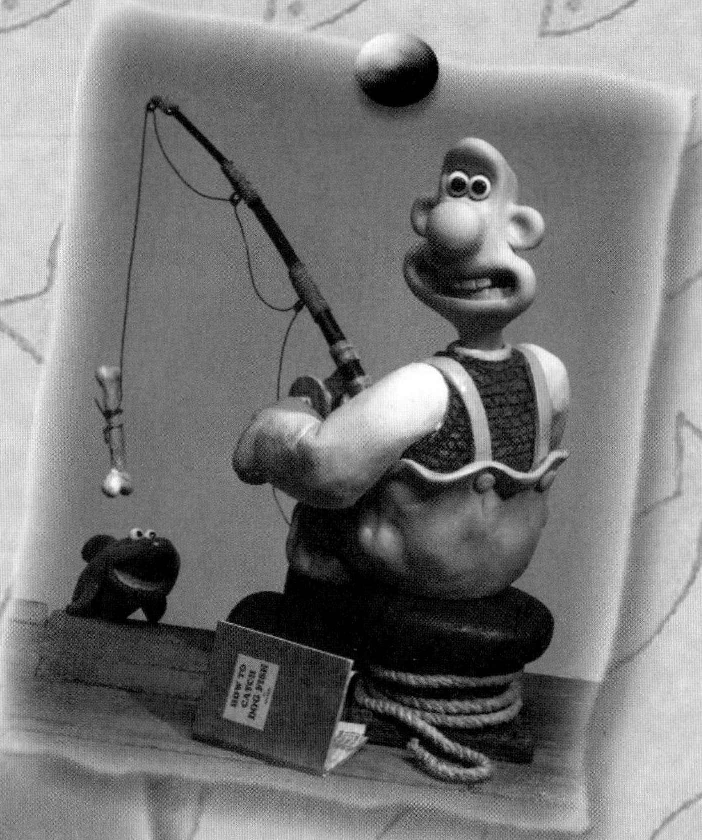
HOW TO CATCH DOG FISH

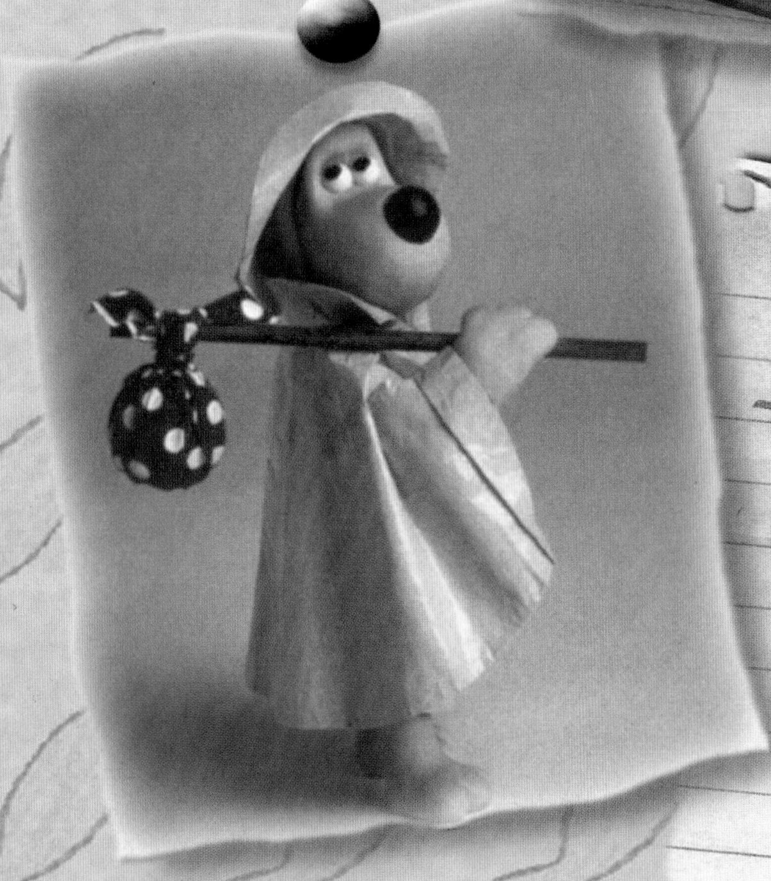

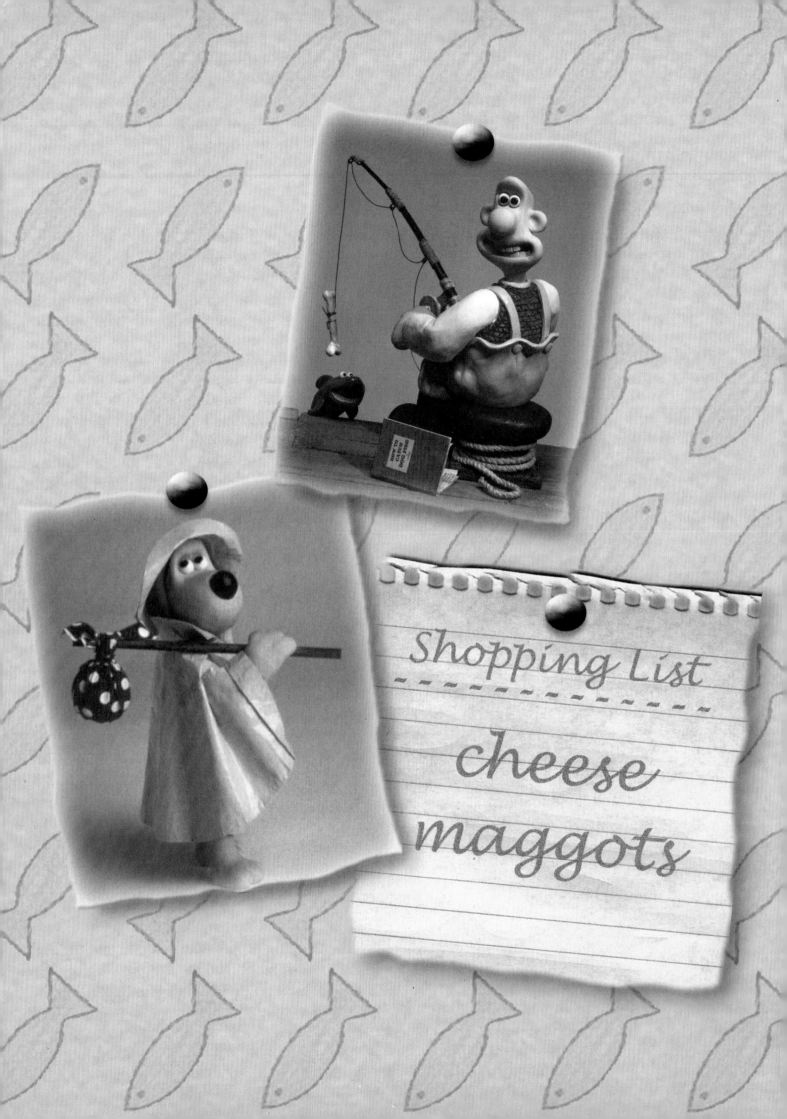

Shopping List

cheese
maggots

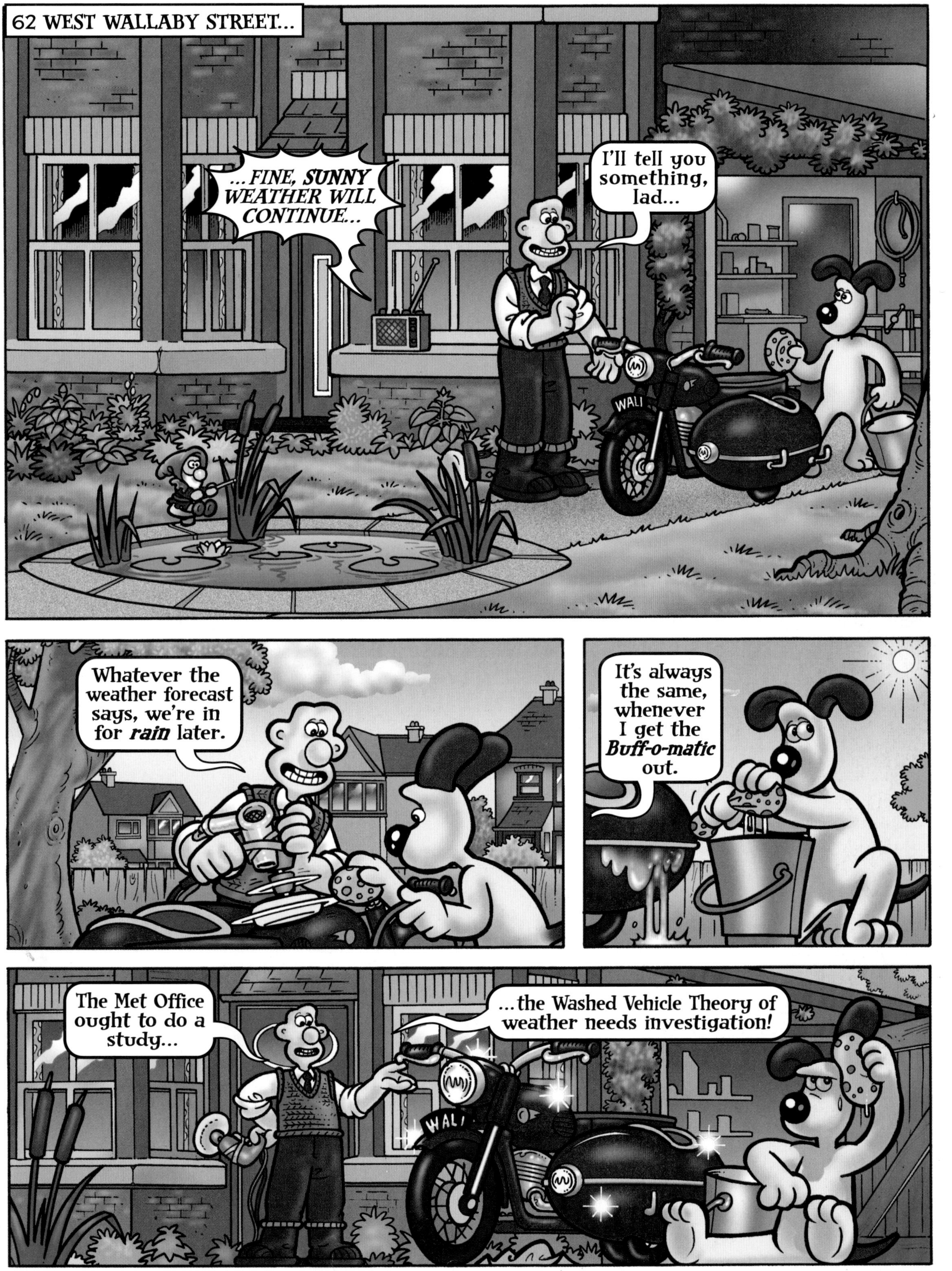
62 WEST WALLABY STREET...
...FINE, SUNNY WEATHER WILL CONTINUE...
I'll tell you something, lad...
Whatever the weather forecast says, we're in for rain later.
It's always the same, whenever I get the Buff-o-matic out.
The Met Office ought to do a study...
...the Washed Vehicle Theory of weather needs investigation!
WALI
WALI

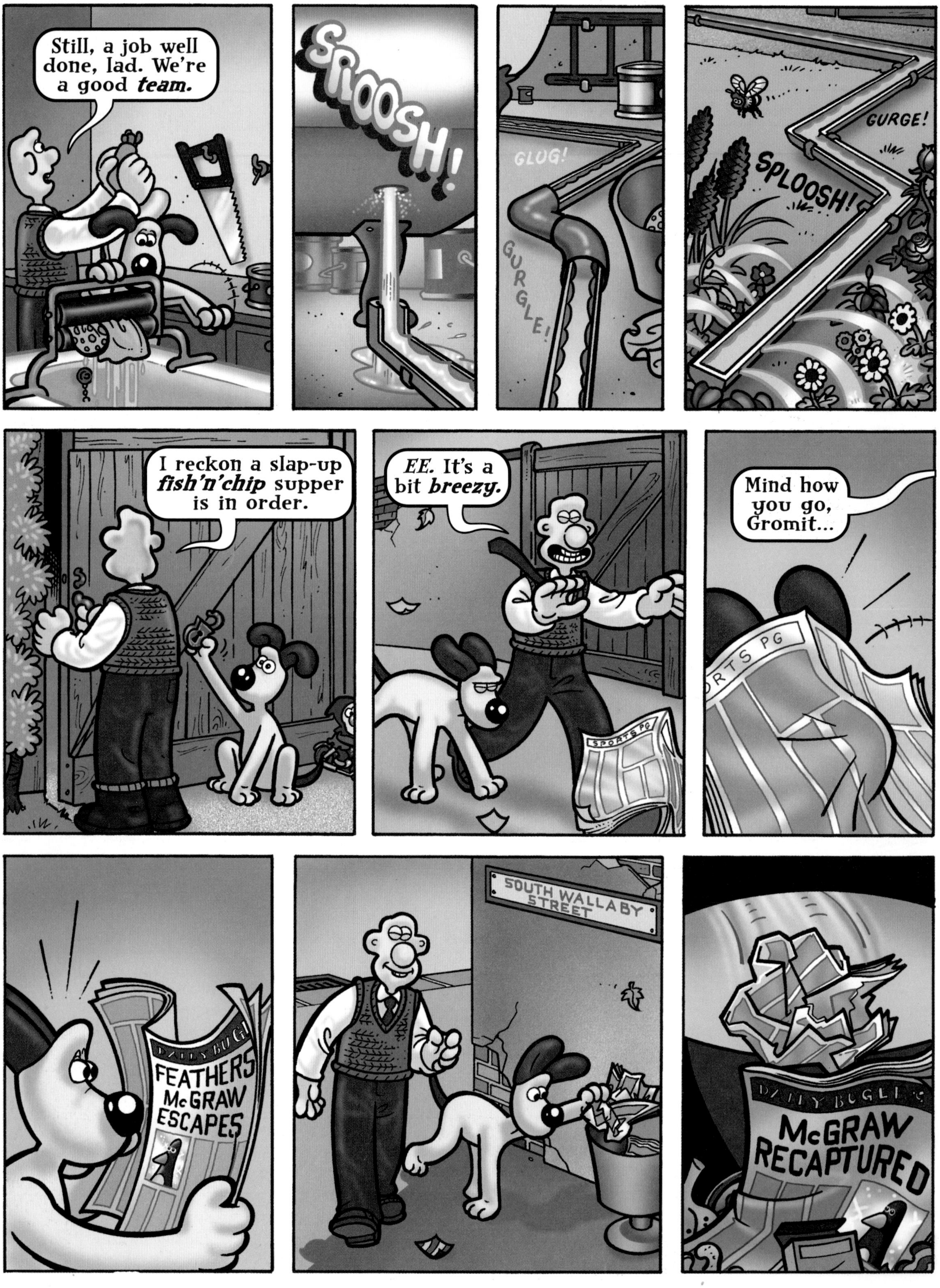

Still, a job well done, lad. We're a good *team.*
SPLOOSH!
GLUG!
GURGLE!
GURGE!
SPLOOSH!
I reckon a slap-up *fish'n'chip* supper is in order.
EE. It's a bit *breezy.*
SPORTS PG
Mind how you go, Gromit...
FEATHERS McGRAW ESCAPES
SOUTH WALLABY STREET
McGRAW RECAPTURED

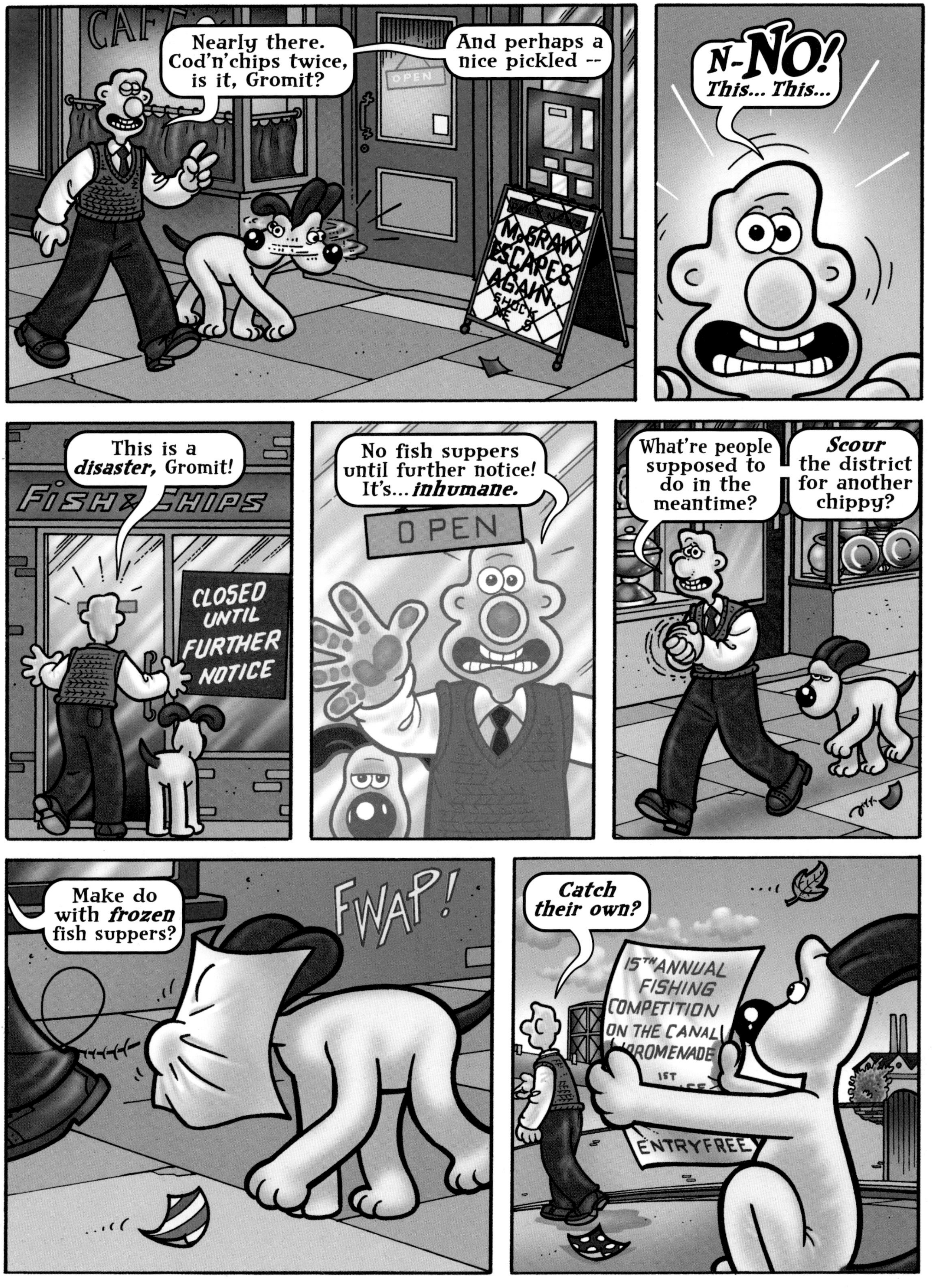
Nearly there. Cod'n'chips twice, is it, Gromit?
And perhaps a nice pickled --
OPEN
McGRAW ESCAPES AGAIN
N-NO! *This... This...*
This is a *disaster,* Gromit!
CLOSED UNTIL FURTHER NOTICE
No fish suppers until further notice! It's... *inhumane.*
OPEN
What're people supposed to do in the meantime?
Scour the district for another chippy?
Make do with *frozen* fish suppers?
FWAP!
Catch their own?
15TH ANNUAL FISHING COMPETITION ON THE CANAL
ROMENADE
1ST
ENTRYFREE

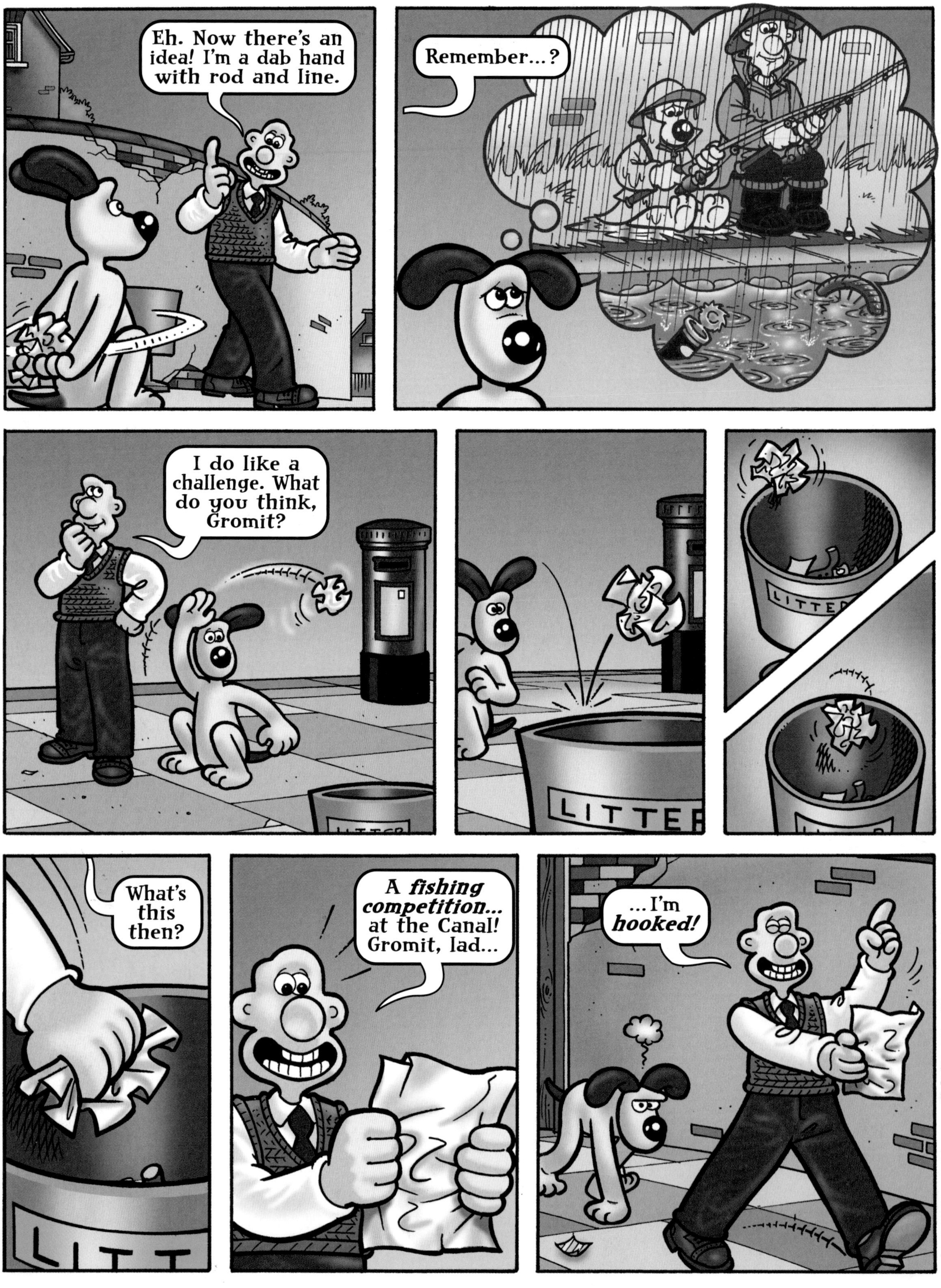

Eh. Now there's an idea! I'm a dab hand with rod and line.
Remember...?
I do like a challenge. What do you think, Gromit?
LITTER
LITTER
What's this then?
LITT
A *fishing* *competition...* at the Canal! Gromit, lad...
...I'm *hooked!*

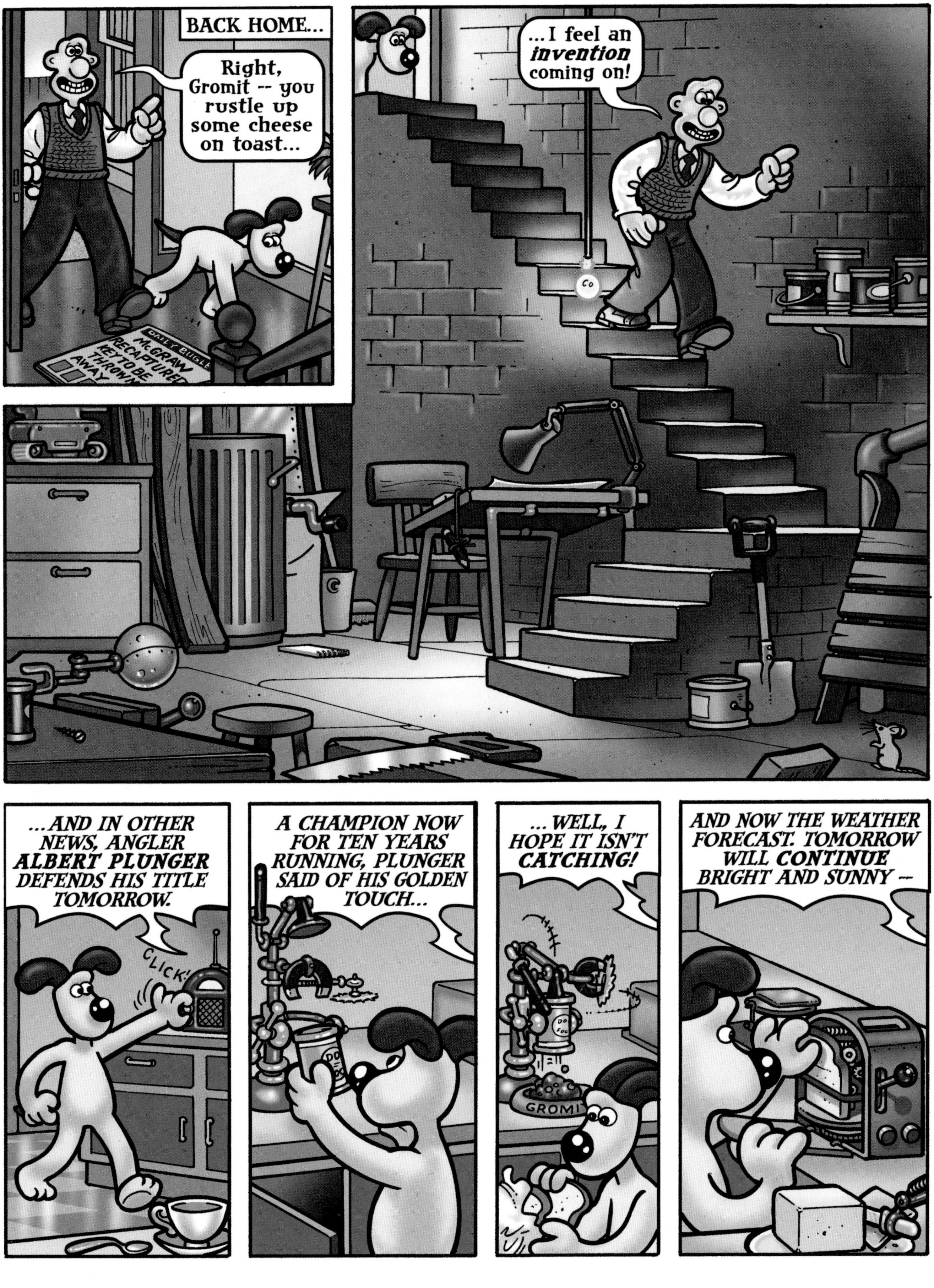

BACK HOME...
Right, Gromit -- you rustle up some cheese on toast...
DAILY BUGLE
McGRAW RECAPTURED
KEY TO BE
...I feel an *invention* coming on!
...AND IN OTHER NEWS, ANGLER **ALBERT PLUNGER** DEFENDS HIS TITLE TOMORROW.
CLICK!
A CHAMPION NOW FOR TEN YEARS RUNNING, PLUNGER SAID OF HIS GOLDEN TOUCH...
... WELL, I HOPE IT ISN'T **CATCHING!**
GROMIT
AND NOW THE WEATHER FORECAST. TOMORROW WILL **CONTINUE** BRIGHT AND SUNNY --

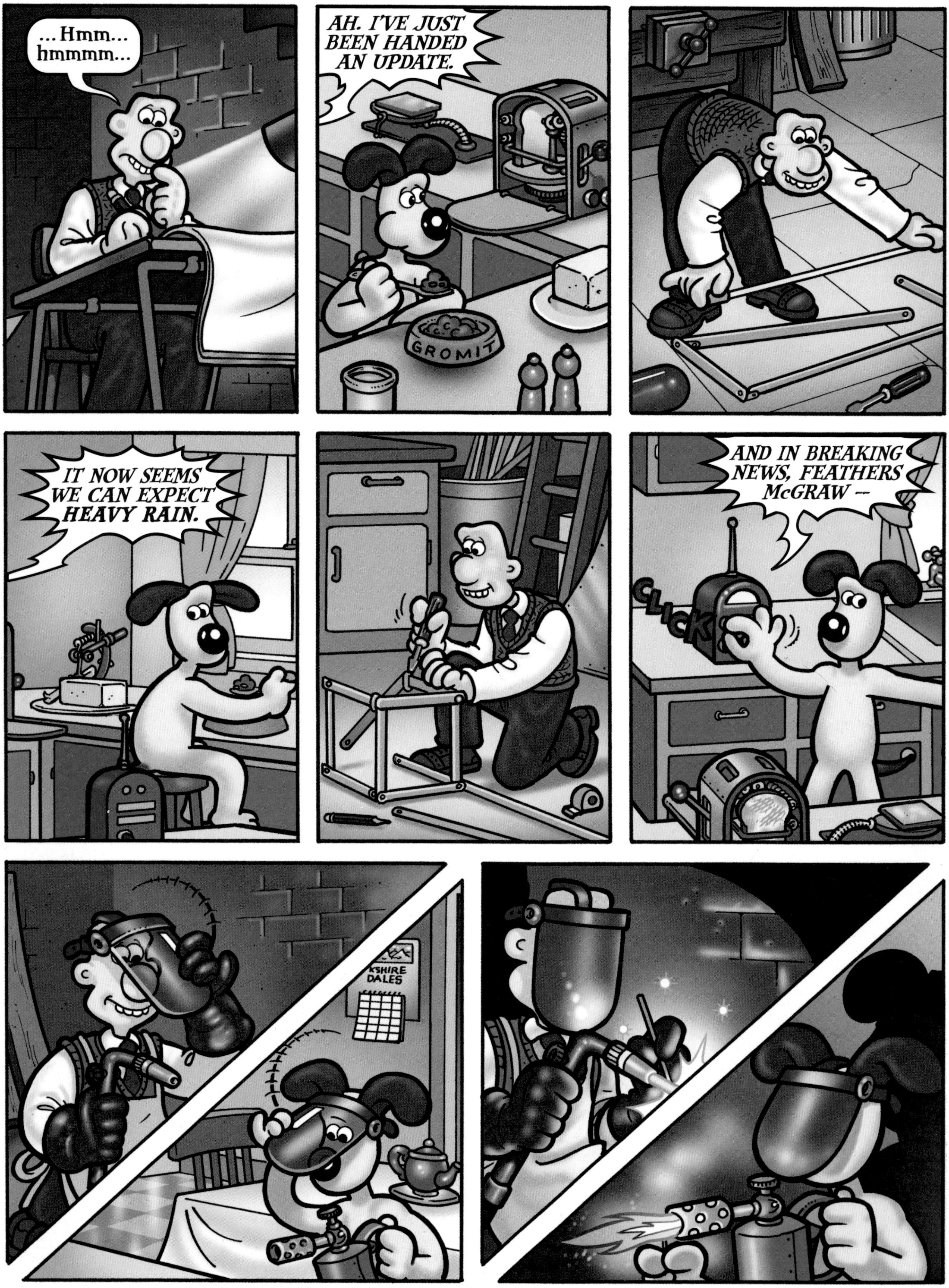
...Hmm...
hmmmm...
AH. I'VE JUST BEEN HANDED AN UPDATE.
GROMIT
IT NOW SEEMS WE CAN EXPECT HEAVY RAIN.
AND IN BREAKING NEWS, FEATHERS McGRAW --
CLICK
KSHIRE DALES

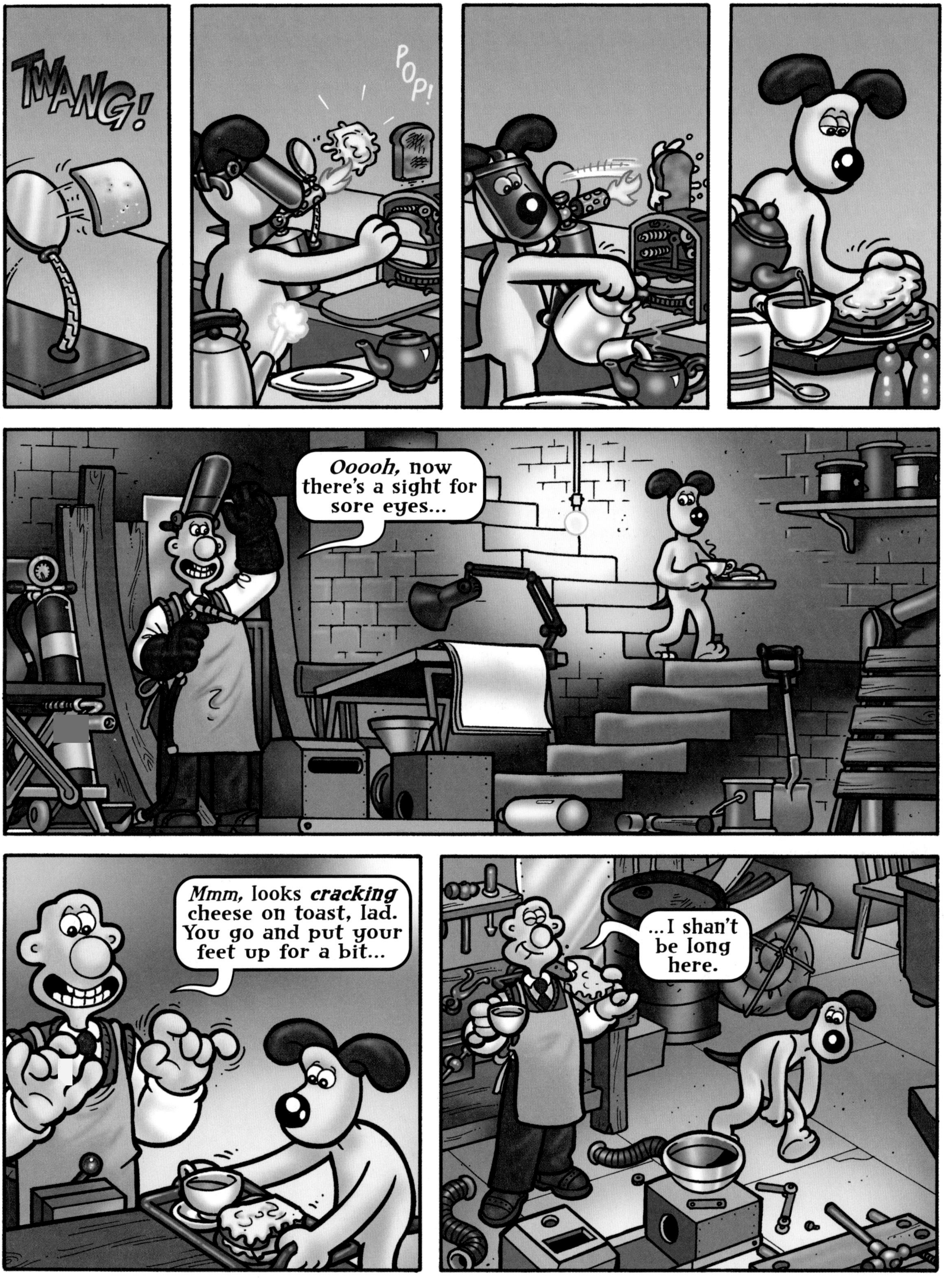

TWANG!
POP!
Ooooh, now there's a sight for sore eyes...
Mmm, looks cracking cheese on toast, lad. You go and put your feet up for a bit...
...I shan't be long here.

SOON...

WHOOSH!!!

CLICK!

BRRRBZZZZZ

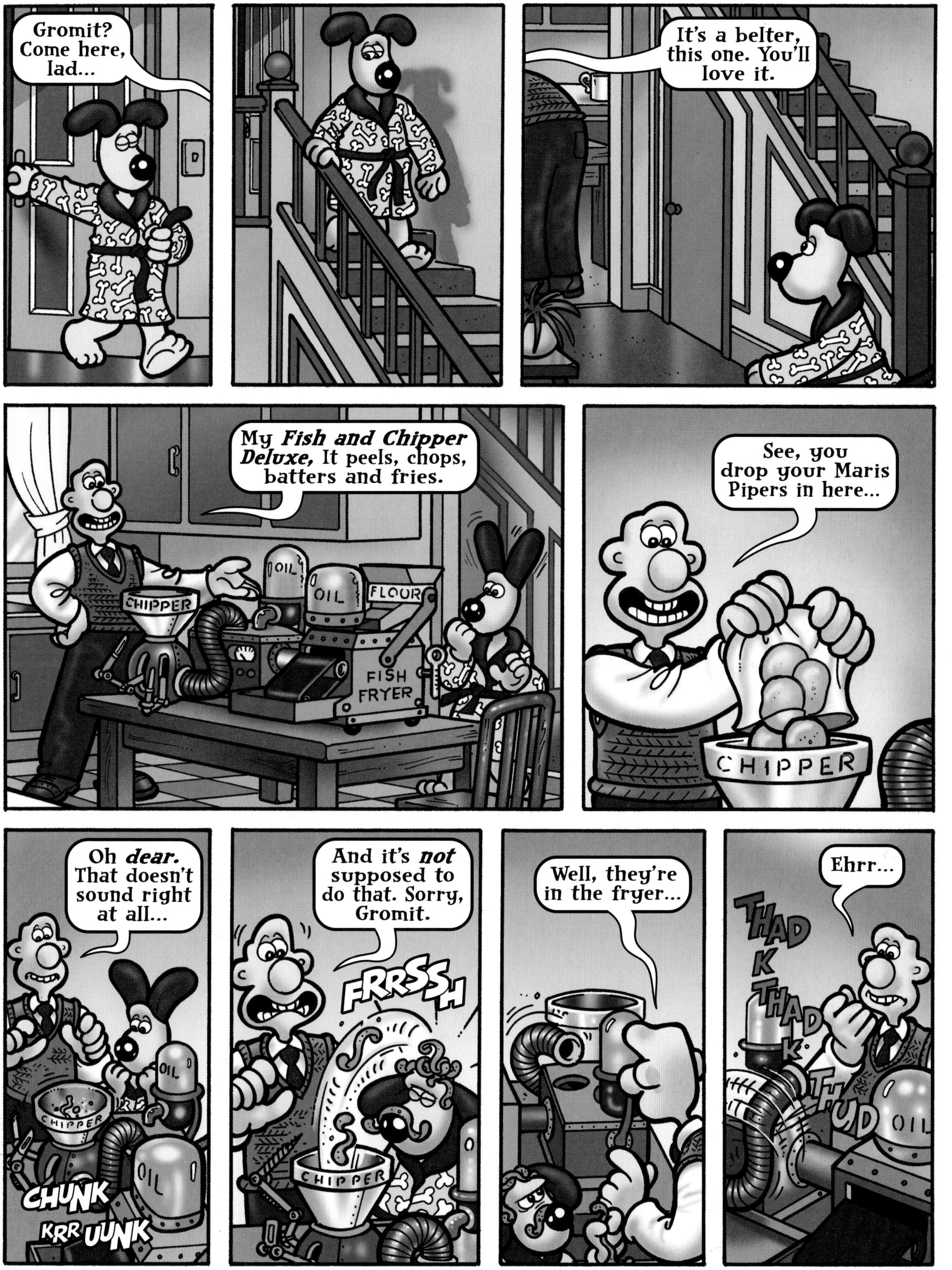
Gromit? Come here, lad...
It's a belter, this one. You'll love it.
My *Fish and Chipper Deluxe,* It peels, chops, batters and fries.
CHIPPER
OIL
OIL
FLOUR
FISH FRYER
See, you drop your Maris Pipers in here...
CHIPPER
Oh *dear.* That doesn't sound right at all...
CHIPPER
OIL
OIL
CHUNK
KRR UUNK
And it's *not* supposed to do that. Sorry, Gromit.
FRRSSH
CHIPPER
Well, they're in the fryer...
Ehrr...
THAD K THAD K THUD
OIL

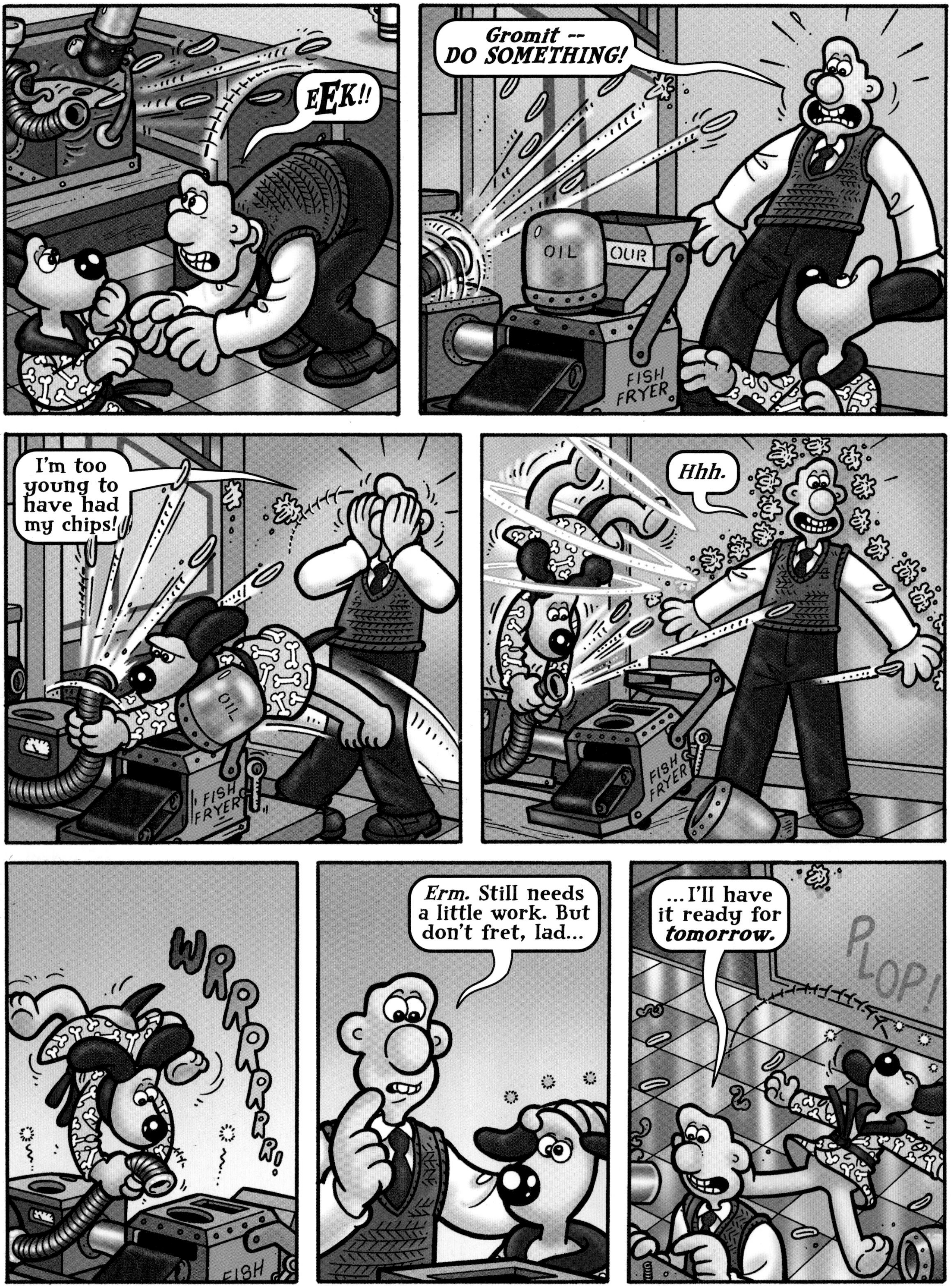
EEK!!
Gromit -- DO SOMETHING!
OIL
OUR
FISH FRYER
I'm too young to have had my chips!
OIL
FISH FRYER
Hhh.
FISH FRYER
WRRRRRR!
FISH
Erm. Still needs a little work. But don't fret, lad...
...I'll have it ready for tomorrow.
PLOP!

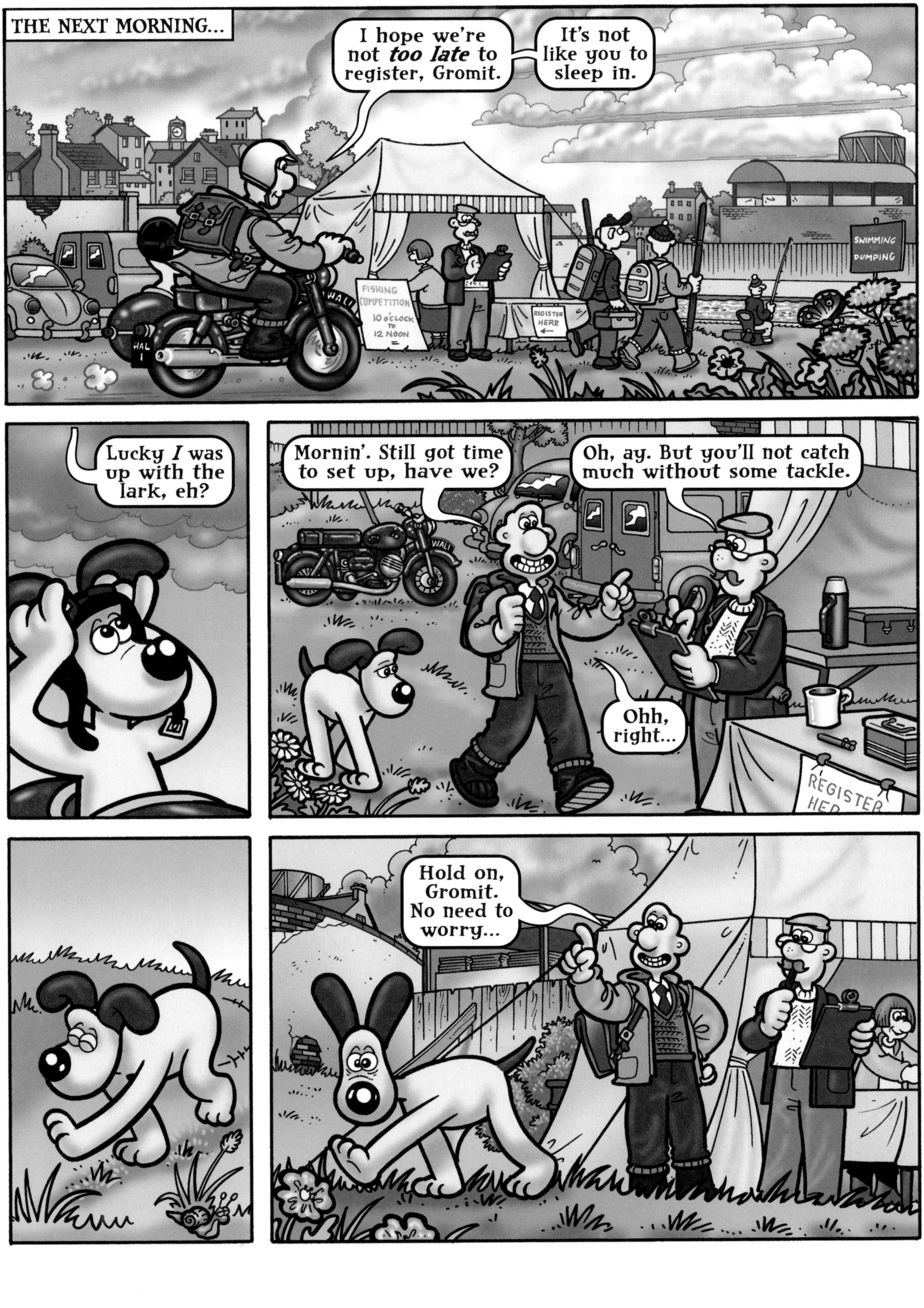
THE NEXT MORNING...
I hope we're not *too late* to register, Gromit.
It's not like you to sleep in.
FISHING COMPETITION 10 o'CLOCK TO 12 NOON
REGISTER HERE
SWIMMING
DUMPING
WAL 1
Lucky *I* was up with the lark, eh?
Mornin'. Still got time to set up, have we?
Oh, ay. But you'll not catch much without some tackle.
Ohh, right...
REGISTER HER
Hold on, Gromit. No need to worry...

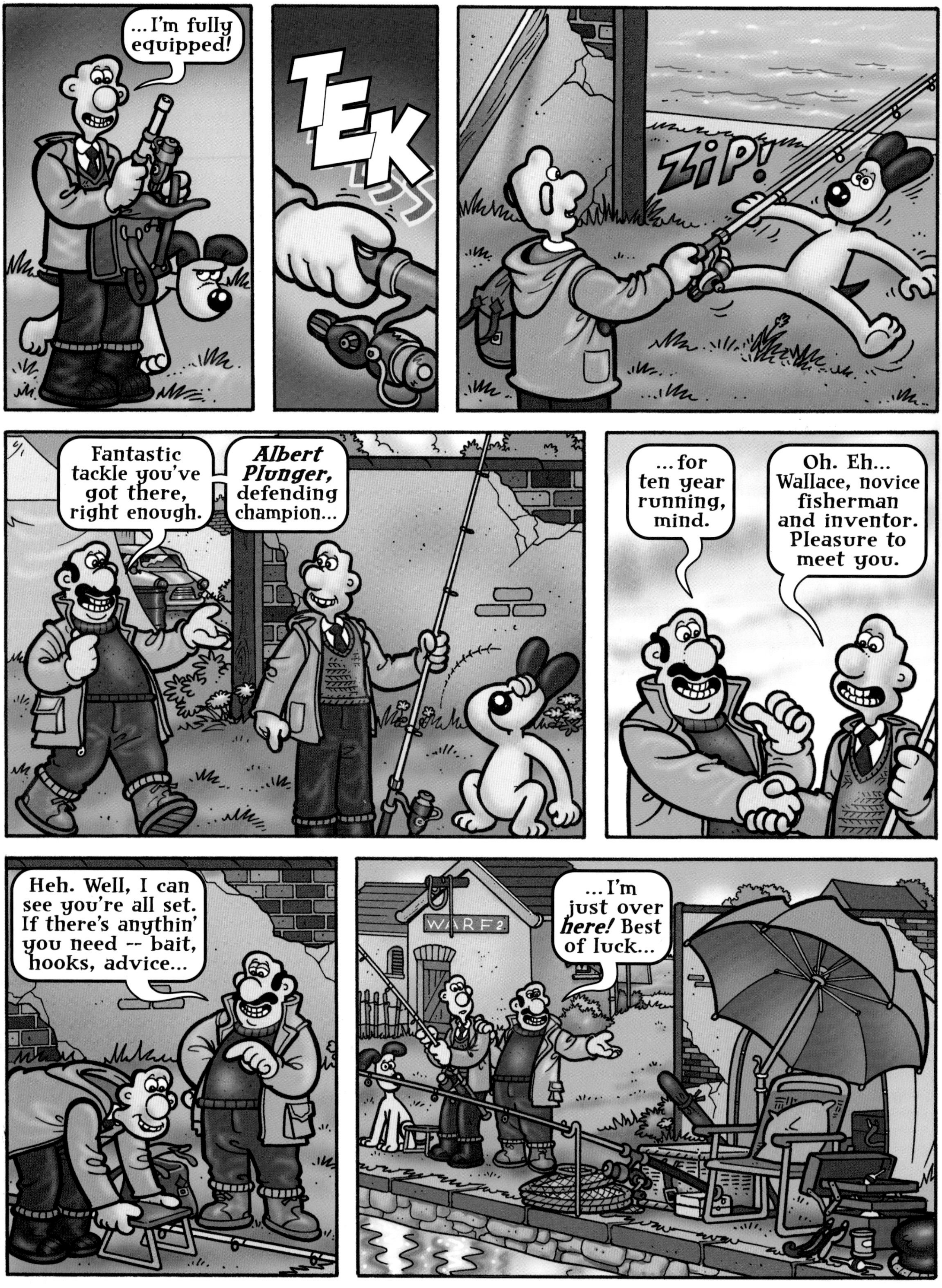
...I'm fully equipped!
TEK
ZIP!
Fantastic tackle you've got there, right enough.
Albert Plunger, defending champion...
...for ten year running, mind.
Oh. Eh... Wallace, novice fisherman and inventor. Pleasure to meet you.
Heh. Well, I can see you're all set. If there's anythin' you need -- bait, hooks, advice...
WARF 2
...I'm just over *here!* Best of luck...

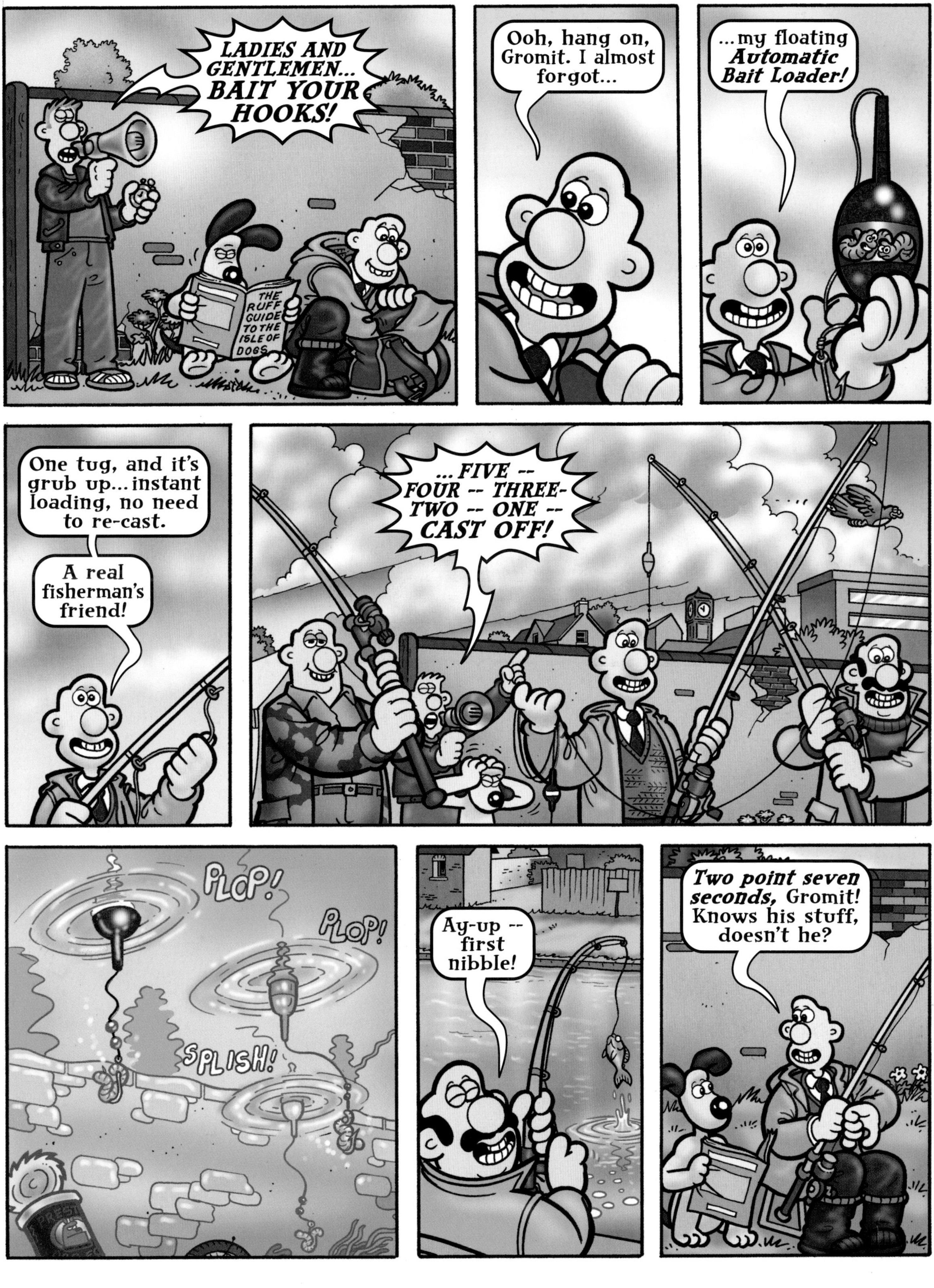
LADIES AND GENTLEMEN... BAIT YOUR HOOKS!
THE RUFF GUIDE TO THE ISLE OF DOGS
Ooh, hang on, Gromit. I almost forgot...
...my floating *Automatic Bait Loader!*
One tug, and it's grub up... instant loading, no need to re-cast.
A real fisherman's friend!
...FIVE -- FOUR -- THREE- TWO -- ONE -- CAST OFF!
PLOP!
PLOP!
SPLISH!
Ay-up -- first nibble!
Two point seven seconds, Gromit! Knows his stuff, doesn't he?

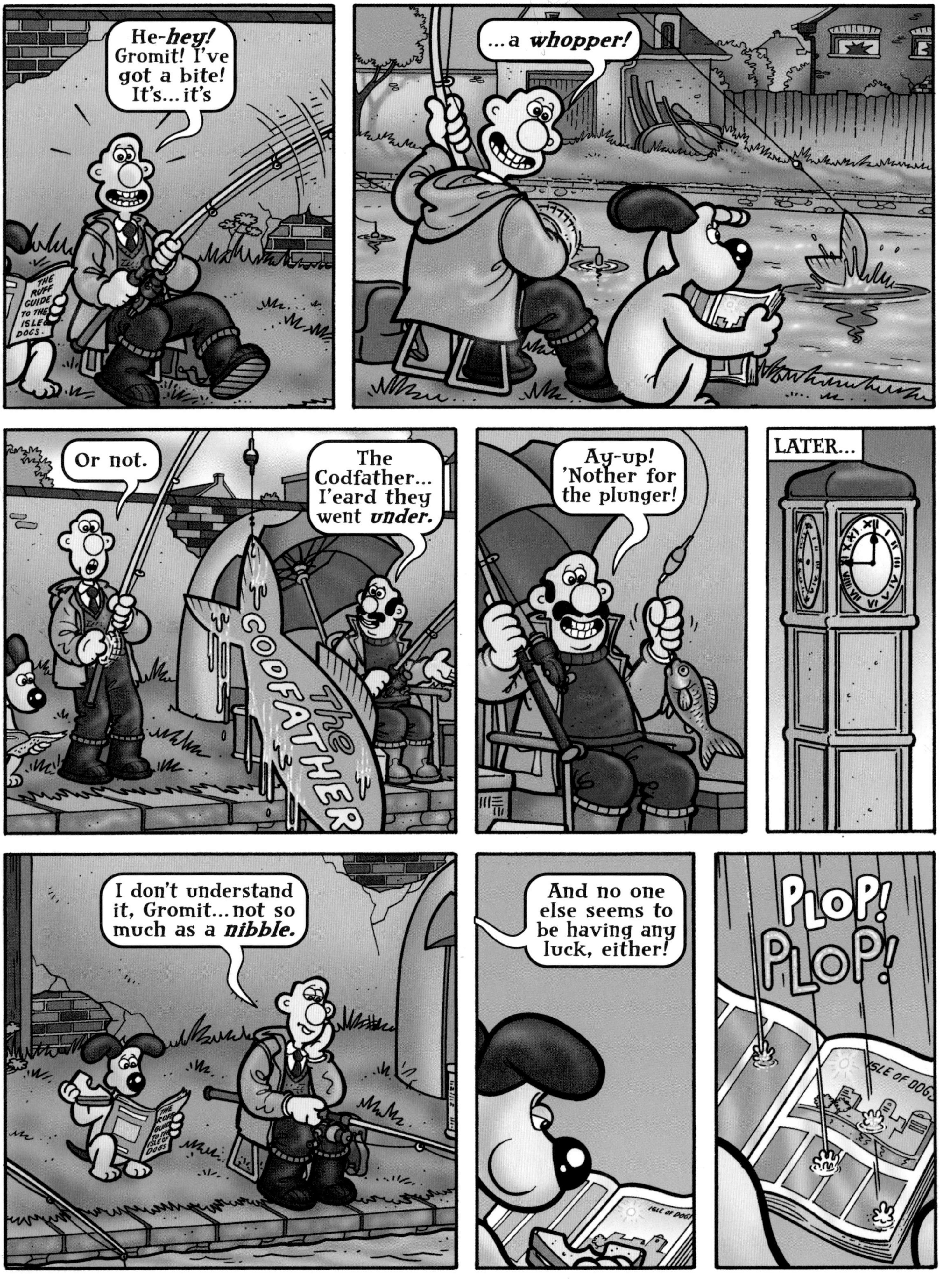

He-*hey!* Gromit! I've got a bite! It's... it's
THE RUFF GUIDE TO THE ISLE DOGS.
...a *whopper!*
Or not.
The Codfather... I'eard they went *under.*
The CODFATHER
Ay-up! 'Nother for the plunger!
LATER...
I don't understand it, Gromit... not so much as a *nibble.*
THE RUFF GUIDE TO THE ISLE OF DOGS
And no one else seems to be having any luck, either!
ISLE OF DOGS
PLOP! PLOP!
ISLE OF DOGS

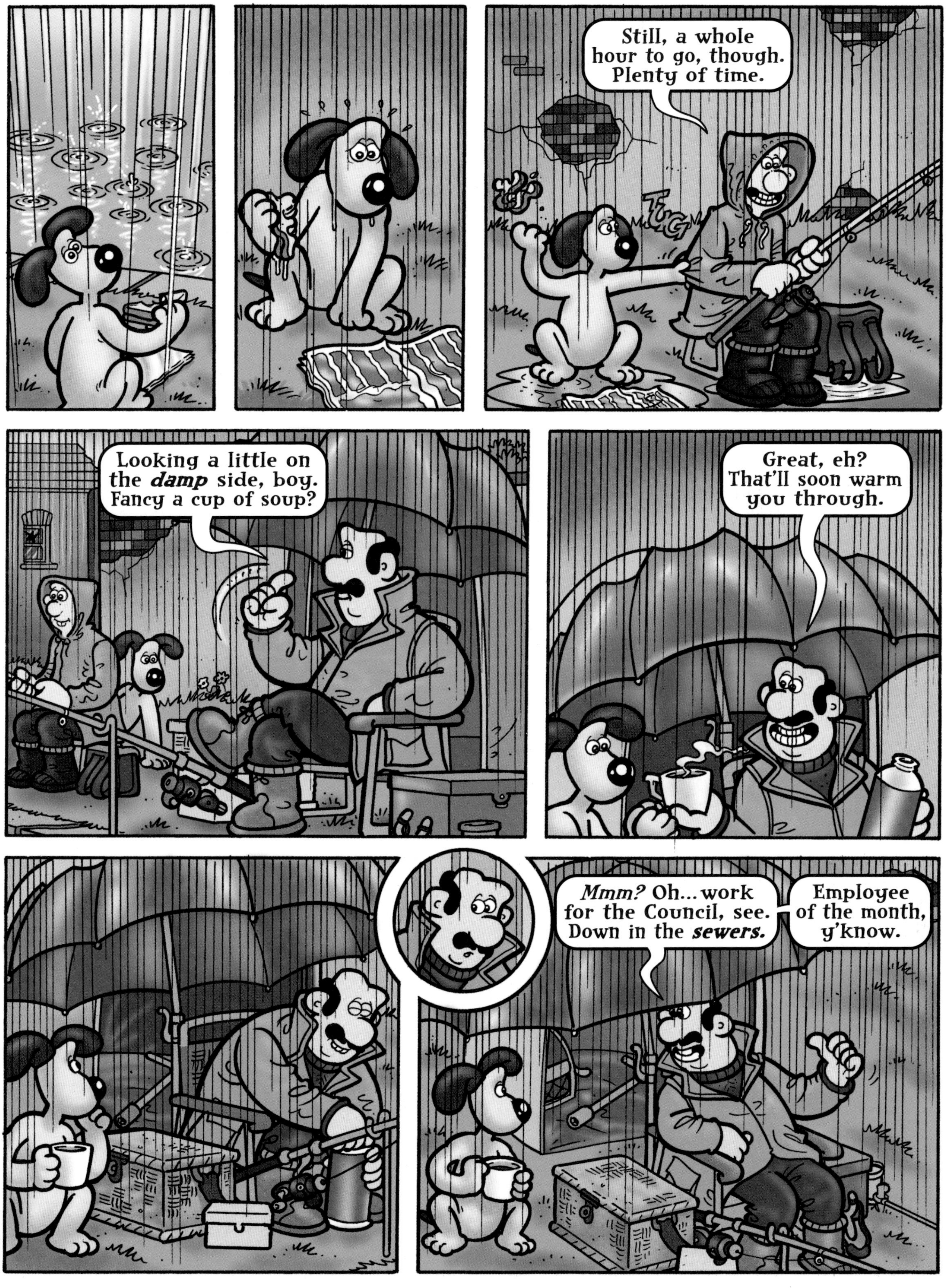
Still, a whole hour to go, though. Plenty of time.
TUG
Looking a little on the *damp* side, boy. Fancy a cup of soup?
Great, eh? That'll soon warm you through.
Mmm? Oh... work for the Council, see. Down in the *sewers.*
Employee of the month, y'know.

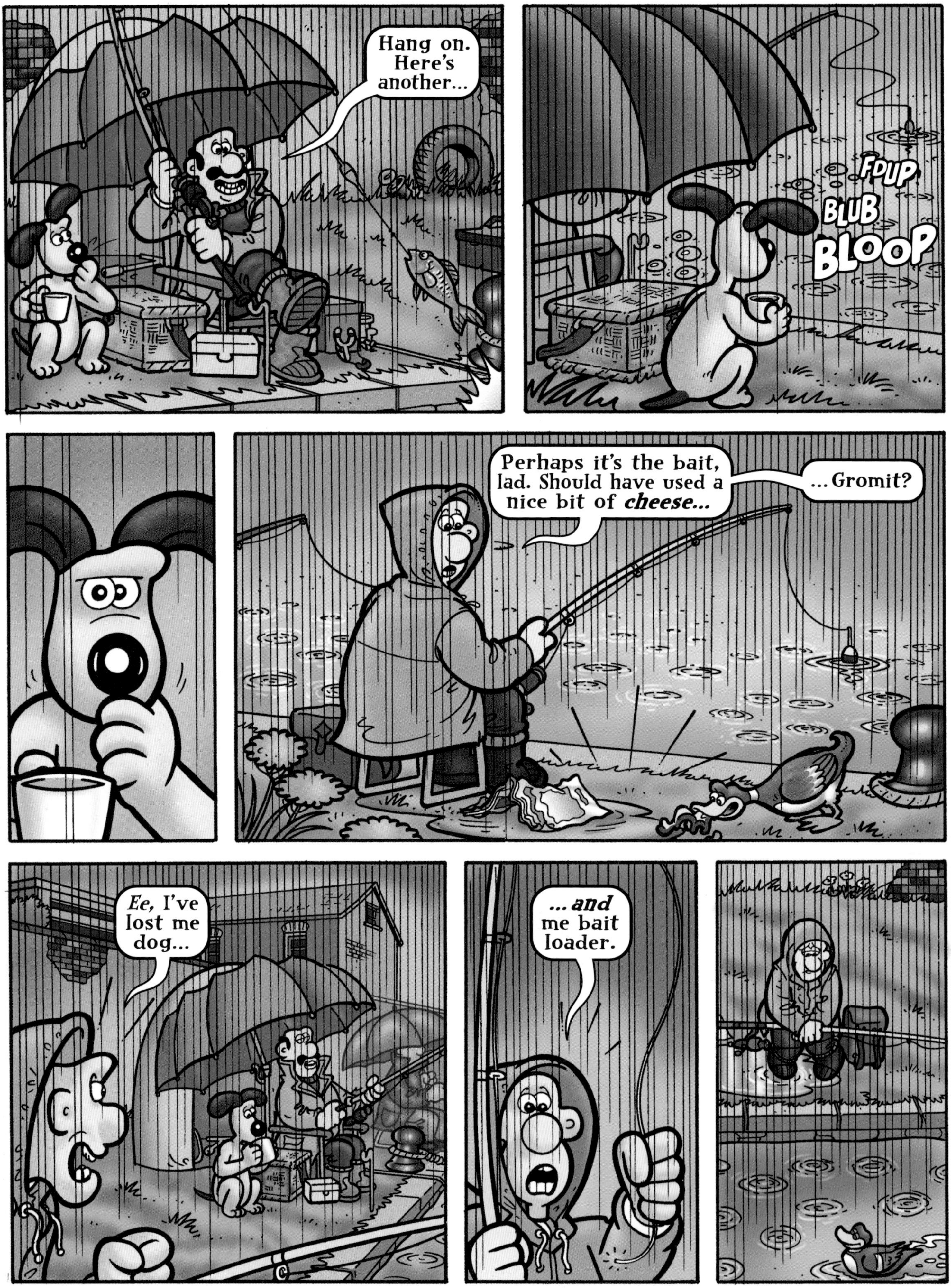
Hang on. Here's another...
FDUP
BLUB
BLOOP
Perhaps it's the bait, lad. Should have used a nice bit of *cheese*...
...Gromit?
Ee, I've lost me dog...
...and me bait loader.

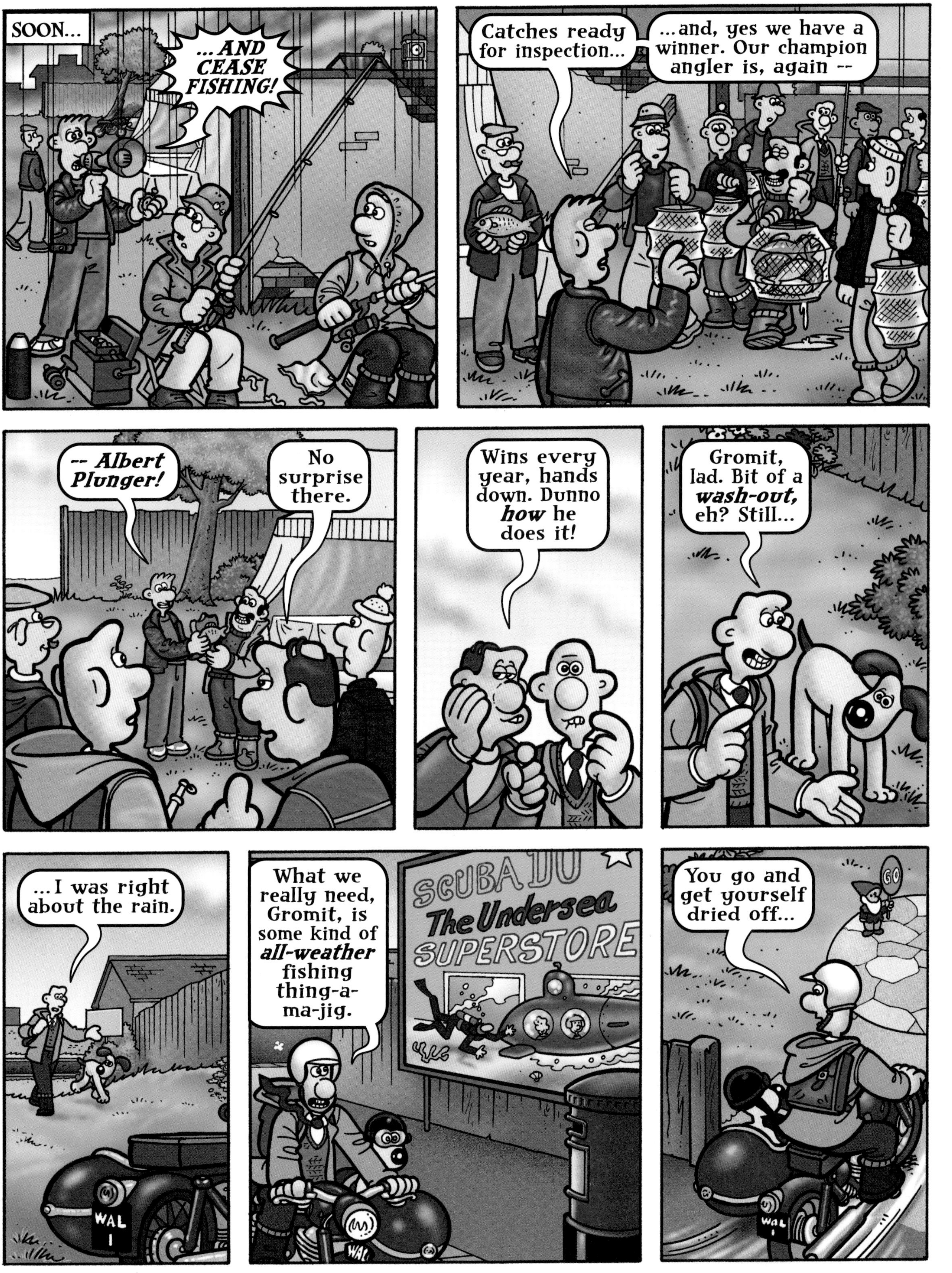
SOON...
...AND CEASE FISHING!
Catches ready for inspection...
...and, yes we have a winner. Our champion angler is, again --
-- Albert Plunger!
No surprise there.
Wins every year, hands down. Dunno how he does it!
Gromit, lad. Bit of a wash-out, eh? Still...
...I was right about the rain.
What we really need, Gromit, is some kind of all-weather fishing thing-a-ma-jig.
SCUBA DU
The Undersea SUPERSTORE
WAL 1
You go and get yourself dried off...
GO

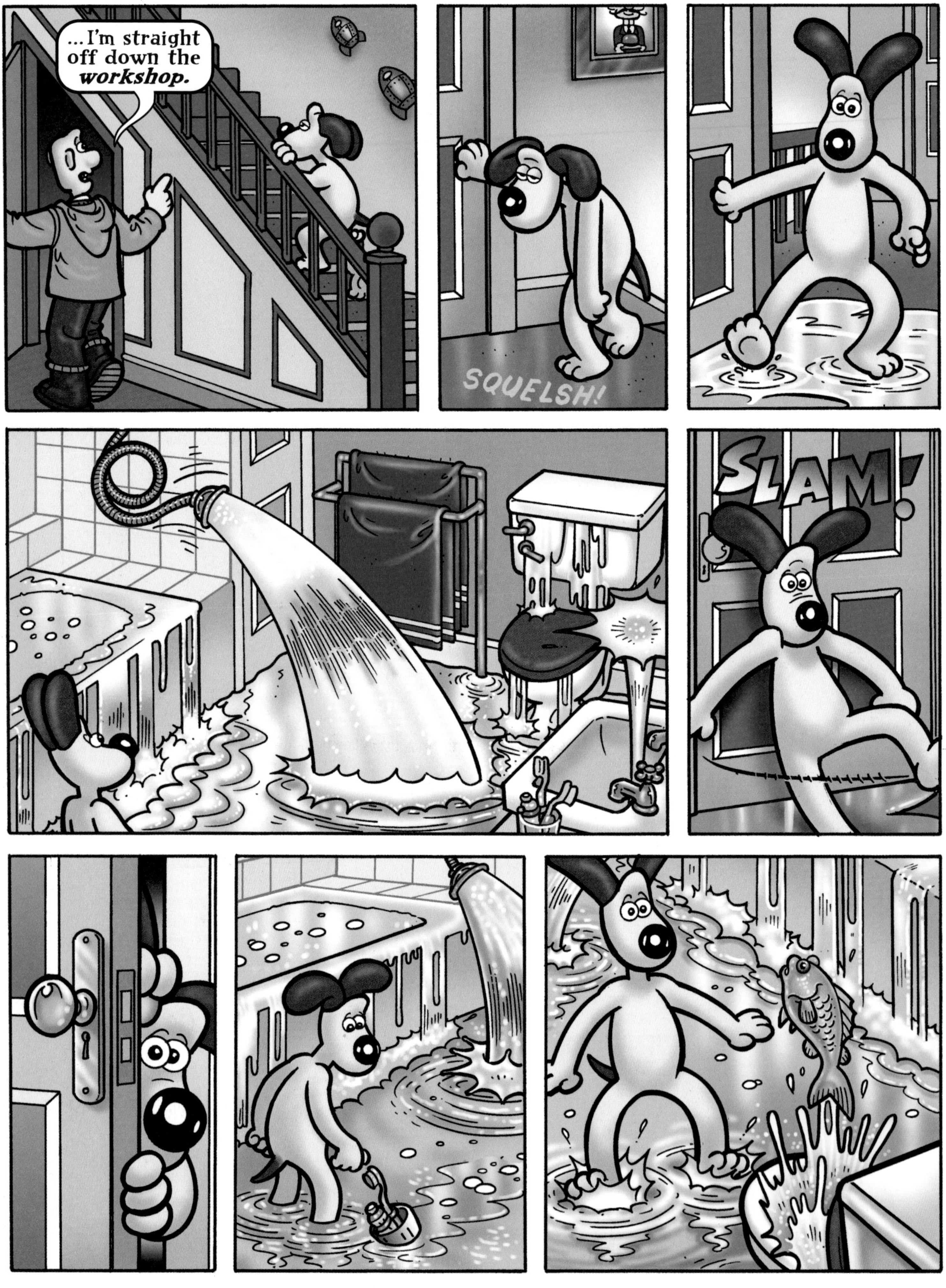
...I'm straight off down the *workshop.*
SQUELSH!
SLAM!

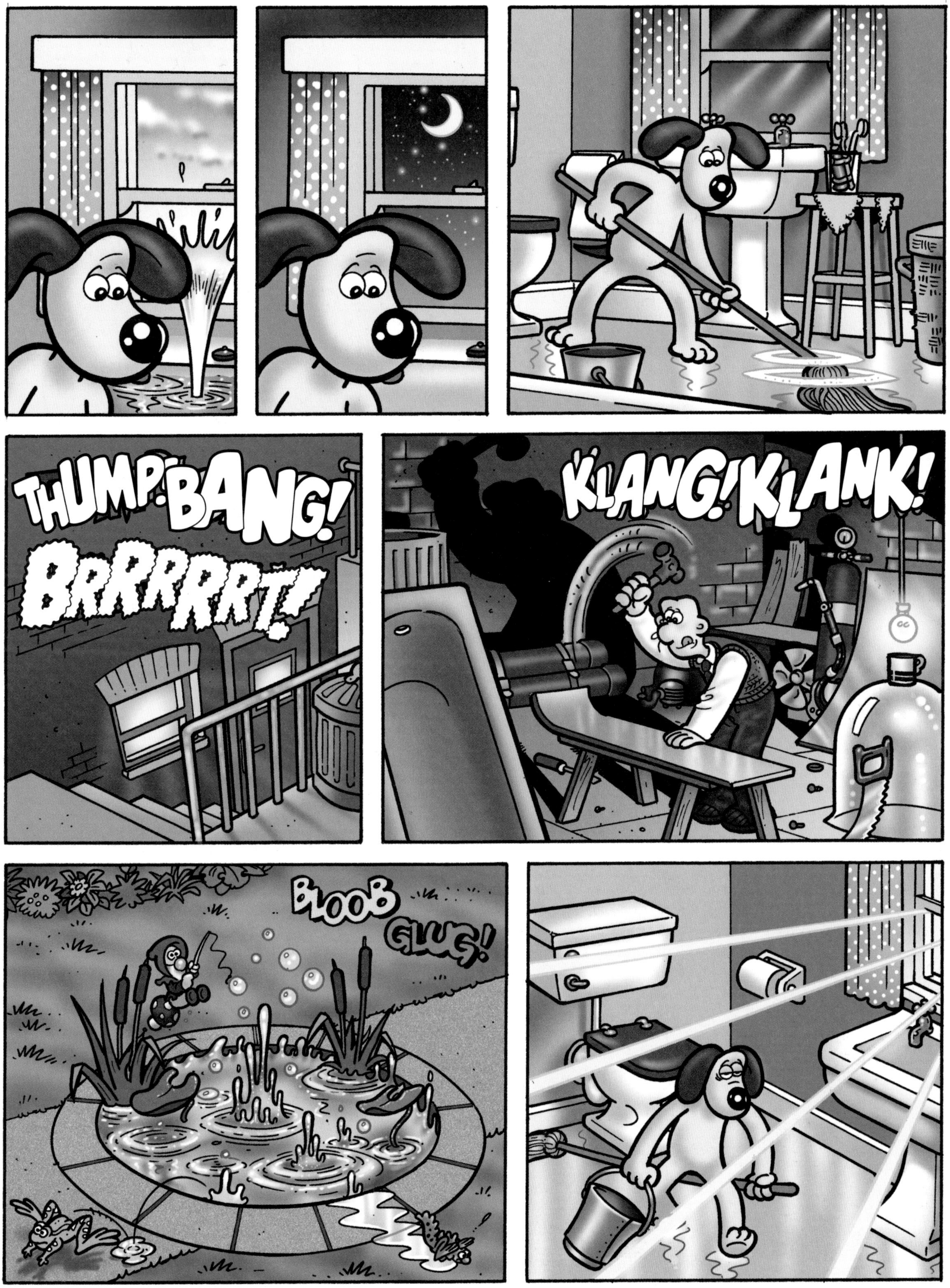
THUMP! BANG!
BRRRRRT!
KLANG! KLANK!
BLOOB
GLUG!

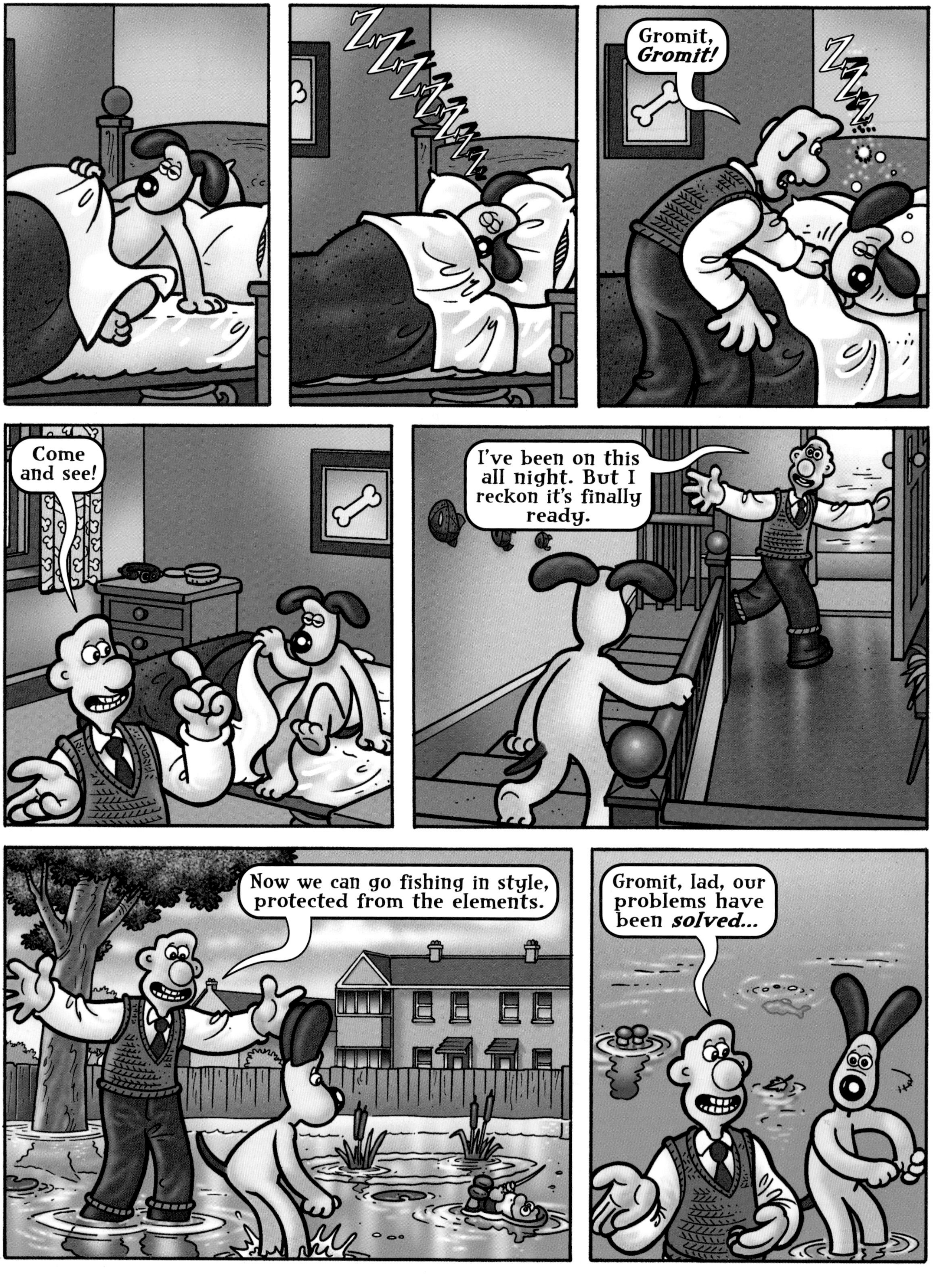

Gromit, *Gromit!*
Come and see!
I've been on this all night. But I reckon it's finally ready.
Now we can go fishing in style, protected from the elements.
Gromit, lad, our problems have been *solved...*

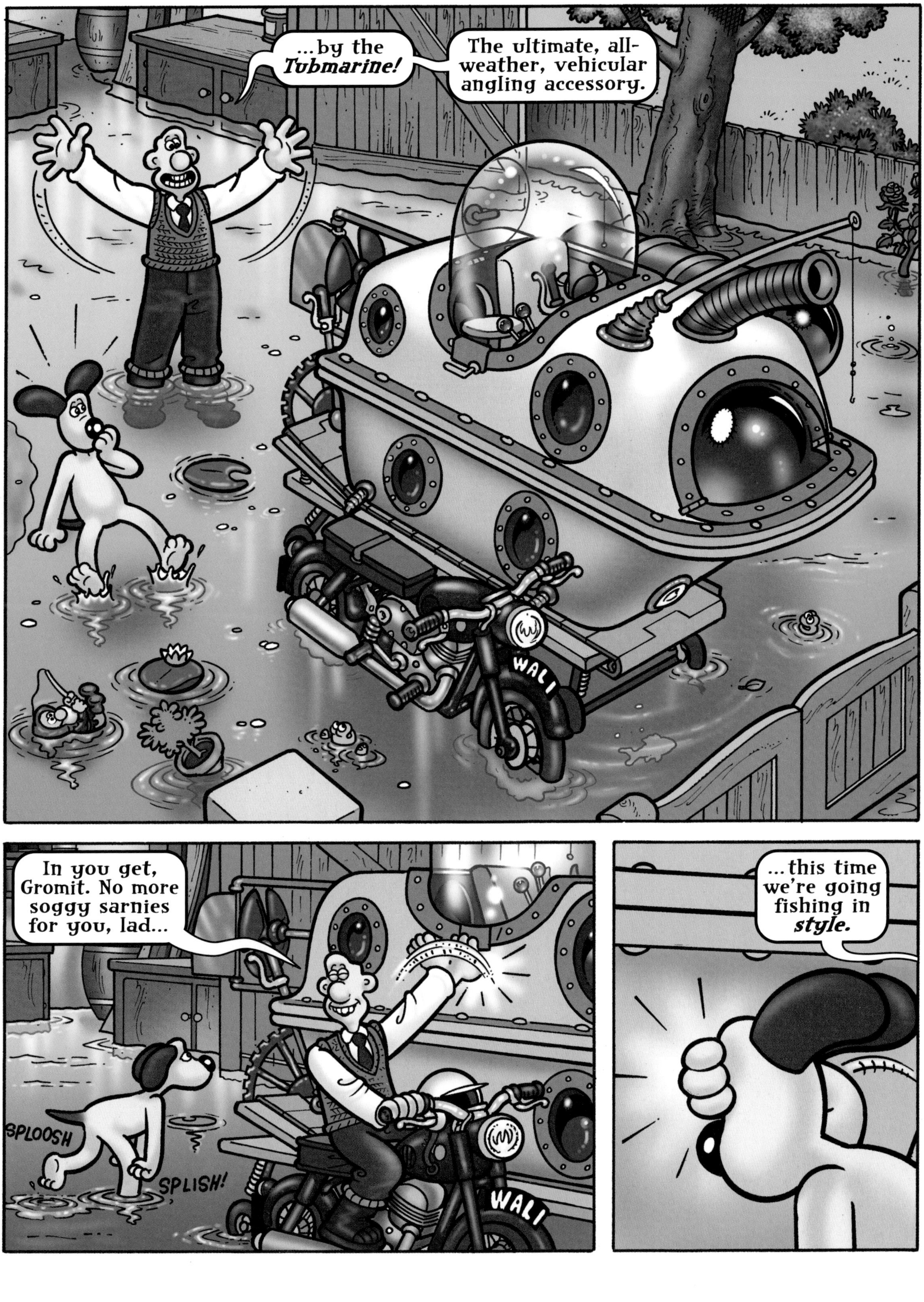
...by the *Tubmarine!*
The ultimate, all-weather, vehicular angling accessory.
WALI
In you get, Gromit. No more soggy sarnies for you, lad...
SPLOOSH
SPLISH!
WALI
...this time we're going fishing in *style.*

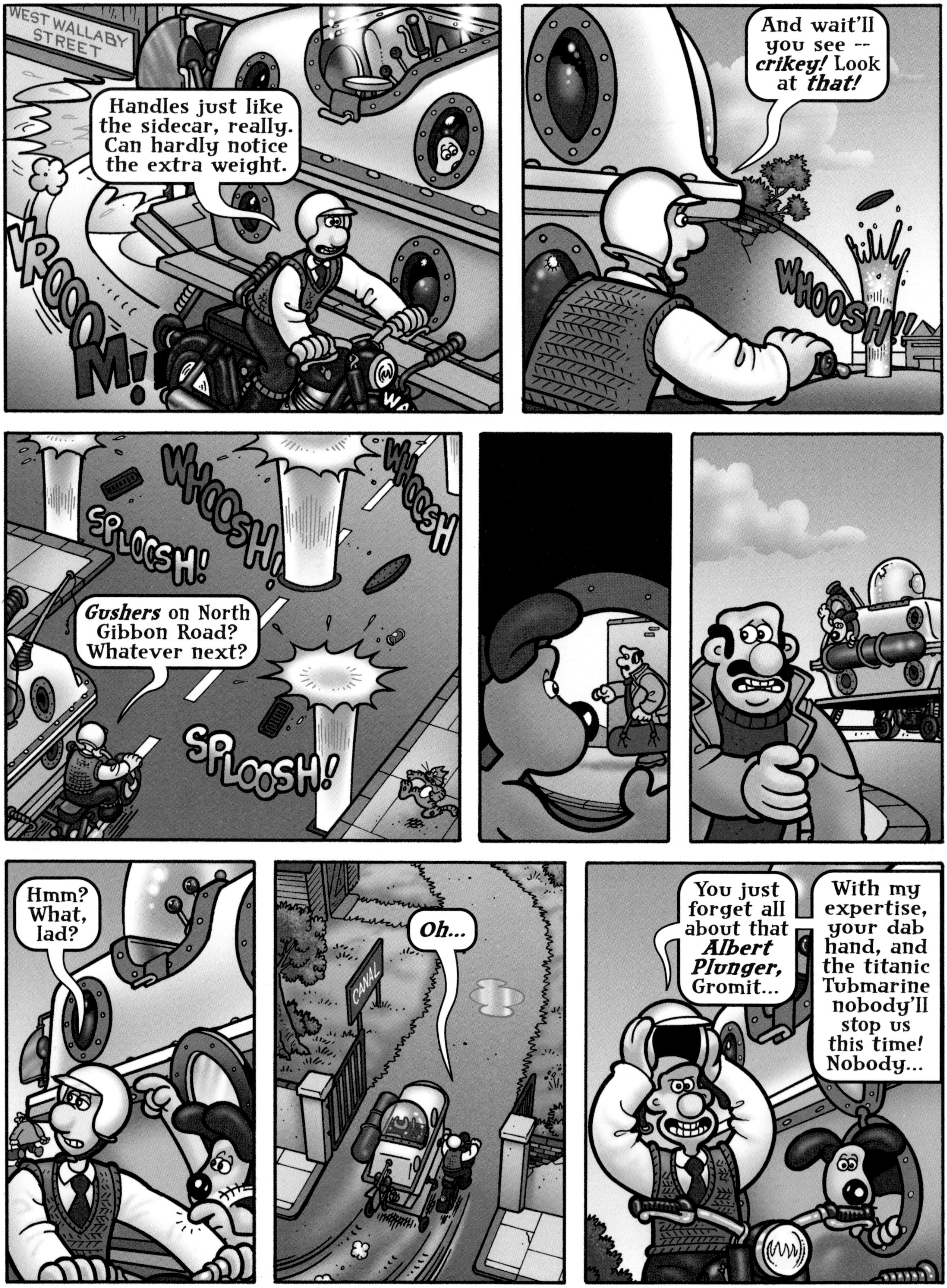
WEST WALLABY STREET
Handles just like the sidecar, really. Can hardly notice the extra weight.
VROOOOM!
And wait'll you see -- *crikey!* Look at ***that!***
WHOOSH!!
WHOOSH
WHOOSH
SPLOOSH!
Gushers on North Gibbon Road? Whatever next?
SPLOOSH!
Hmm? What, lad?
CANAL
Oh...
You just forget all about that ***Albert Plunger,*** Gromit...
With my expertise, your dab hand, and the titanic Tubmarine nobody'll stop us this time! Nobody...

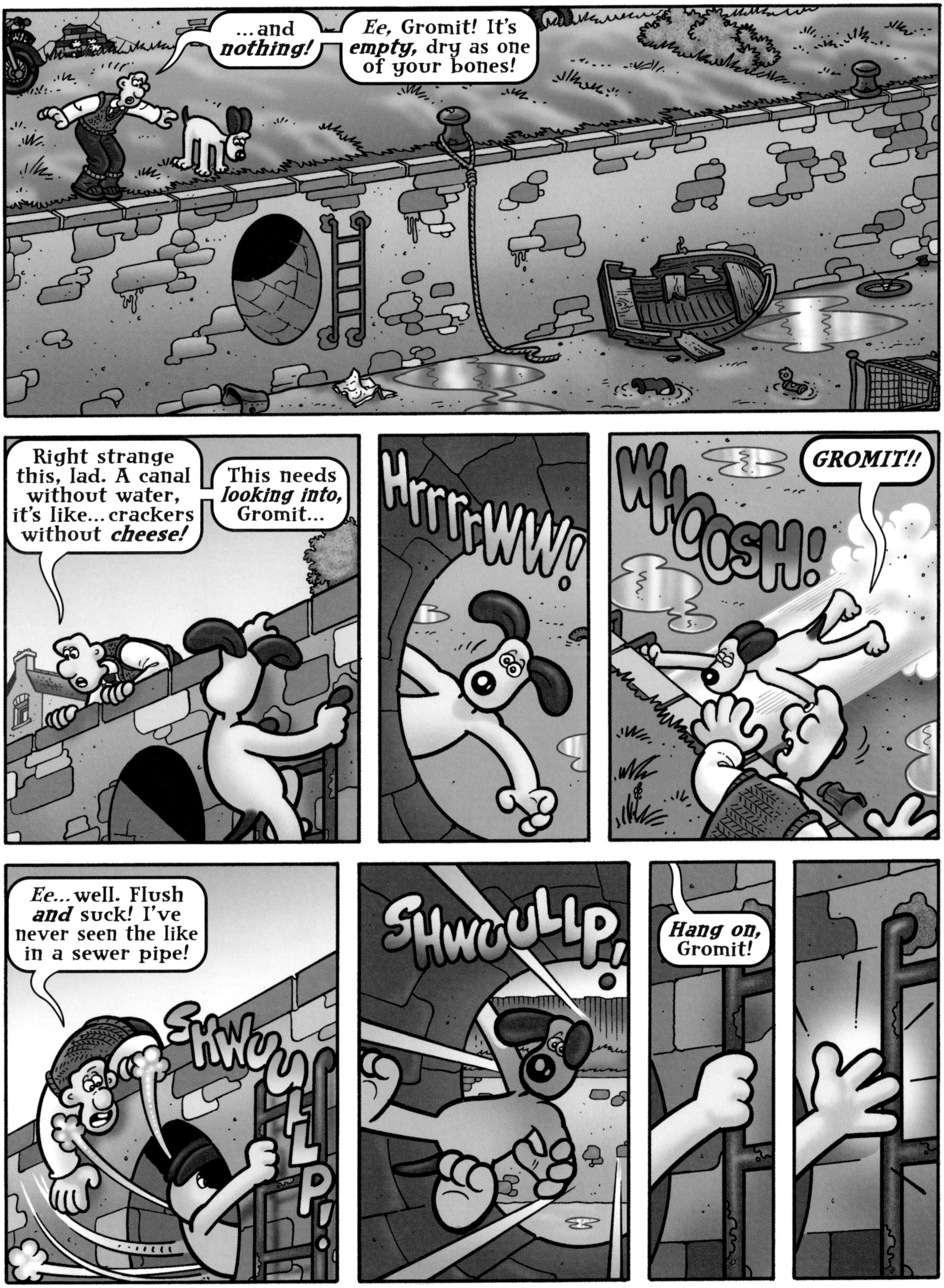

...and *nothing!*
Ee, Gromit! It's *empty,* dry as one of your bones!
Right strange this, lad. A canal without water, it's like... crackers without *cheese!*
This needs *looking into,* Gromit...
HrrrrWW!
WHOOSH!
GROMIT!!
Ee... well. Flush *and* suck! I've never seen the like in a sewer pipe!
SHWUULLP!
SHWUULLP!
Hang on, Gromit!

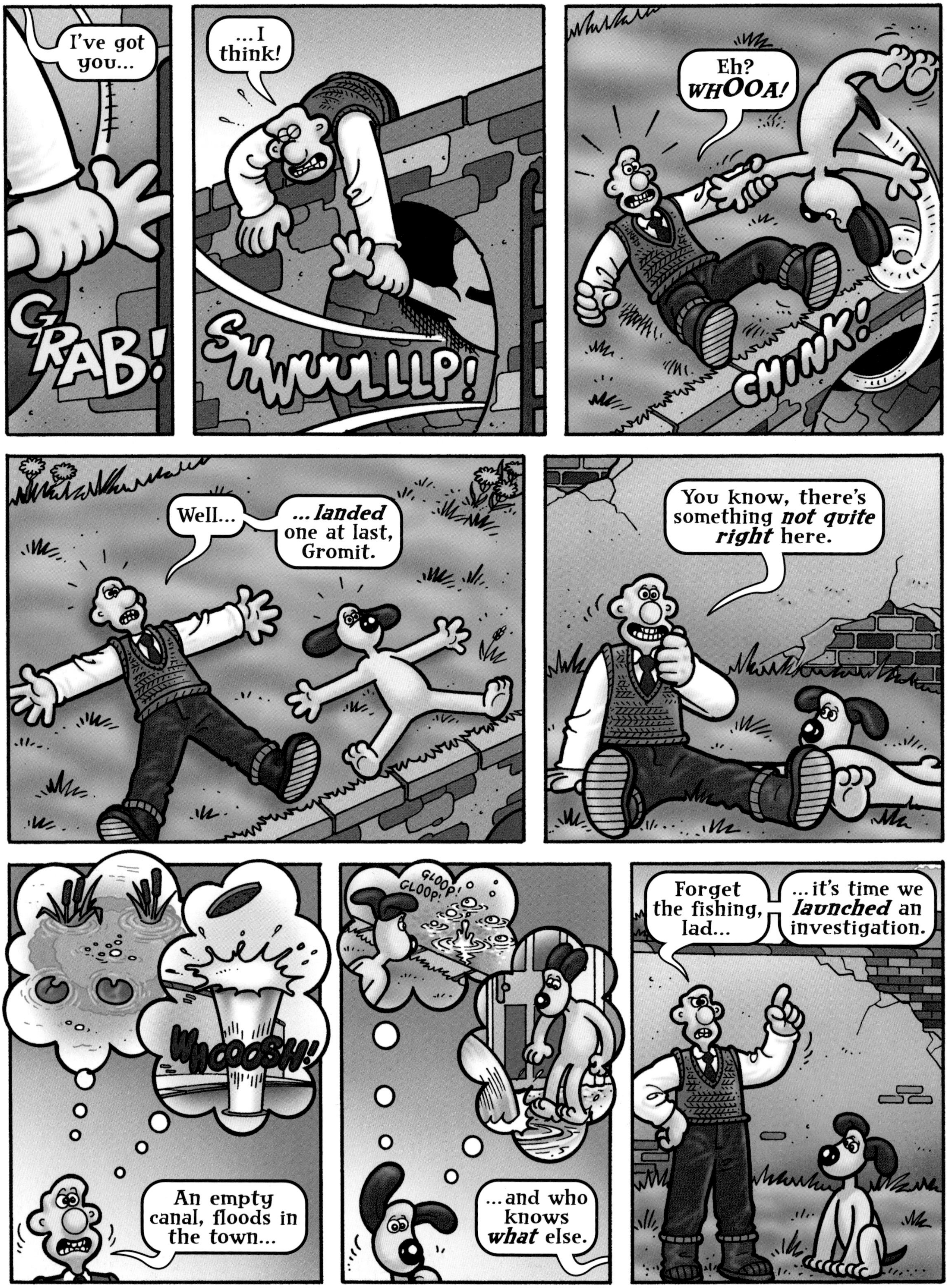

I've got you...
GRAB!
...I think!
SHWUULLLP!
Eh? WHOOA!
CHINK!
Well...
...landed one at last, Gromit.
You know, there's something not quite right here.
WHOOSH!
An empty canal, floods in the town...
GLOOP! GLOOP!
...and who knows what else.
Forget the fishing, lad...
...it's time we launched an investigation.

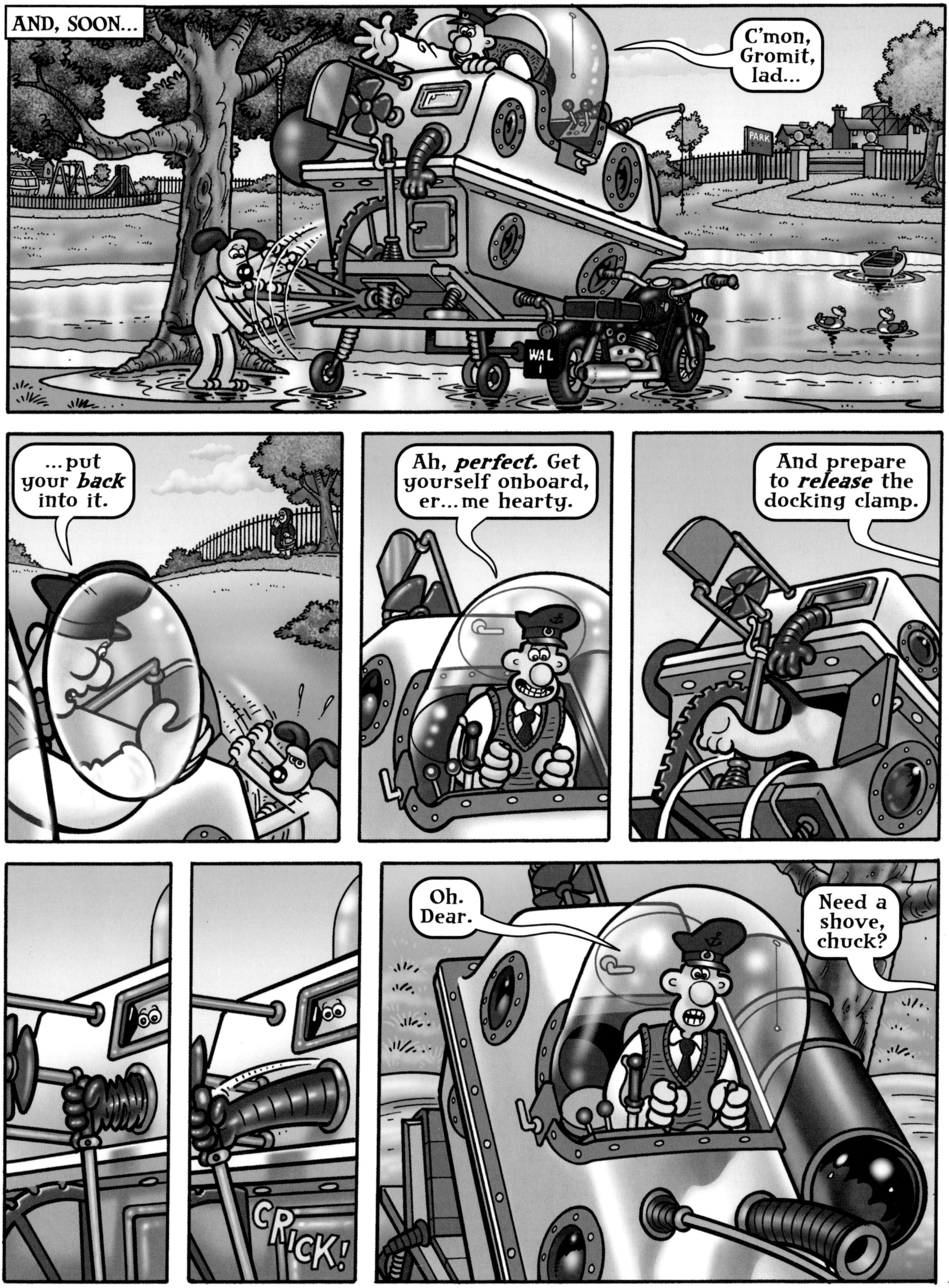
AND, SOON...
C'mon, Gromit, lad...
PARK
WAL 1
...put your *back* into it.
Ah, *perfect.* Get yourself onboard, er...me hearty.
And prepare to *release* the docking clamp.
CRICK!
Oh. Dear.
Need a shove, chuck?

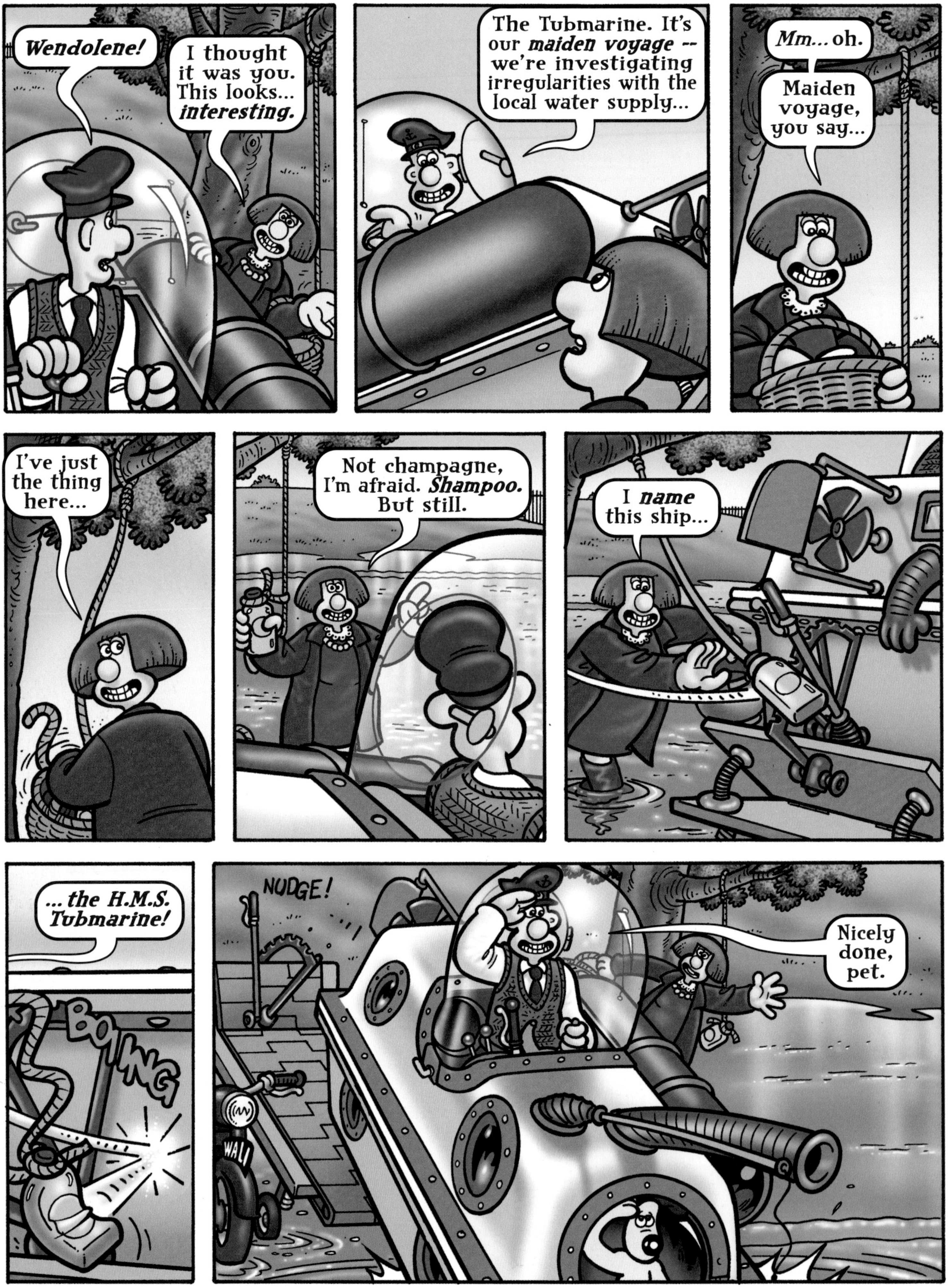
Wendolene!
I thought it was you. This looks... *interesting.*
The Tubmarine. It's our *maiden voyage* -- we're investigating irregularities with the local water supply...
Mm... oh.
Maiden voyage, you say...
I've just the thing here...
Not champagne, I'm afraid. *Shampoo.* But still.
I *name* this ship...
... *the H.M.S. Tubmarine!*
BOING
NUDGE!
Nicely done, pet.
WALl

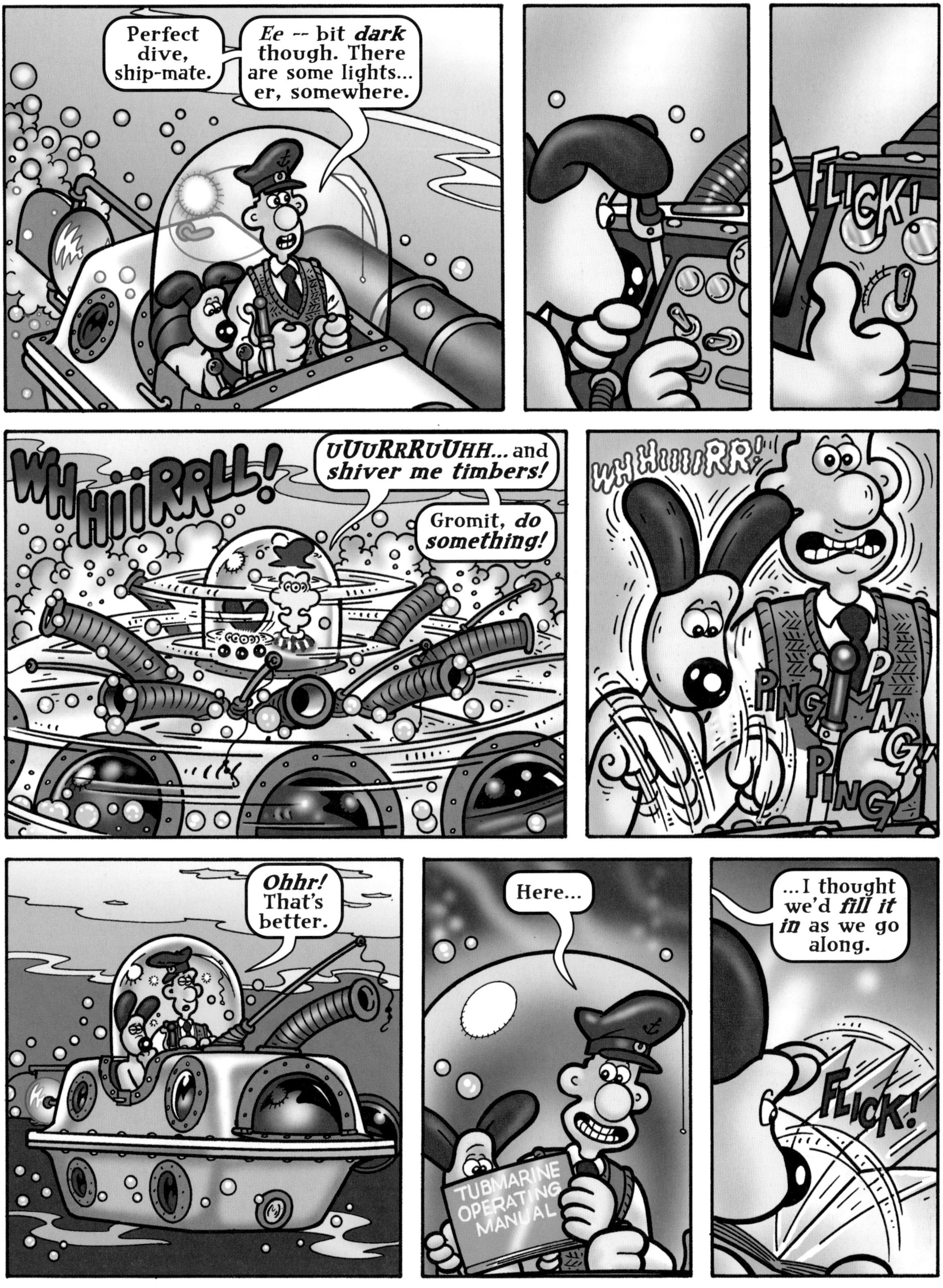

Perfect dive, ship-mate.
Ee -- bit **dark** though. There are some lights... er, somewhere.
FLICK!
WHHIIRRLL!
UUURRRUUHH... and shiver me timbers!
Gromit, *do something!*
WHHIIIRR!
PING! PING! PING! PING!
Ohhr! That's better.
Here...
TUBMARINE OPERATING MANUAL
...I thought we'd *fill it in* as we go along.
FLICK!

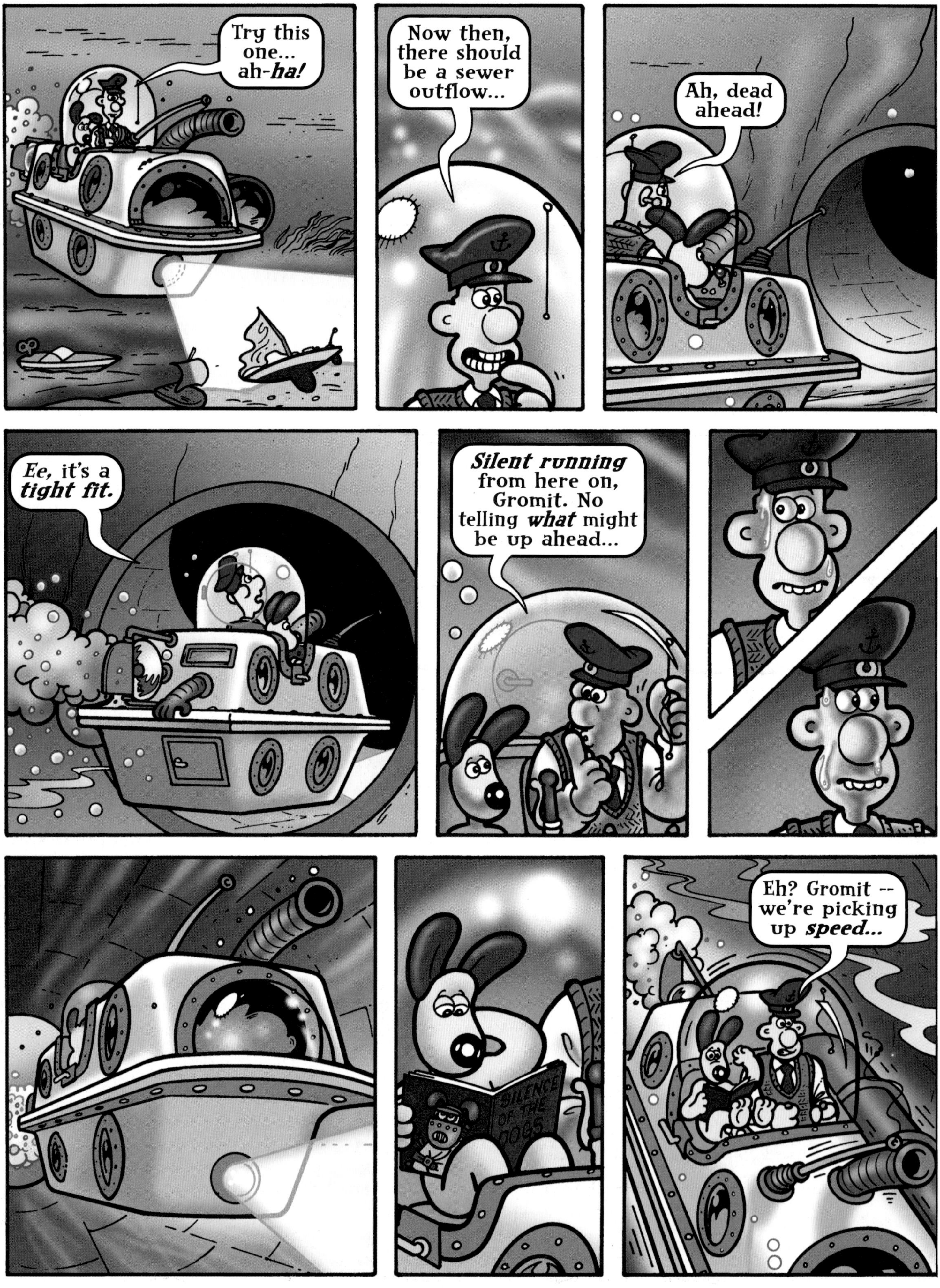

Try this one... ah-*ha!*
Now then, there should be a sewer outflow...
Ah, dead ahead!
Ee, it's a *tight fit.*
Silent running from here on, Gromit. No telling *what* might be up ahead...
SILENCE OF THE DOGS
Eh? Gromit -- we're picking up *speed...*

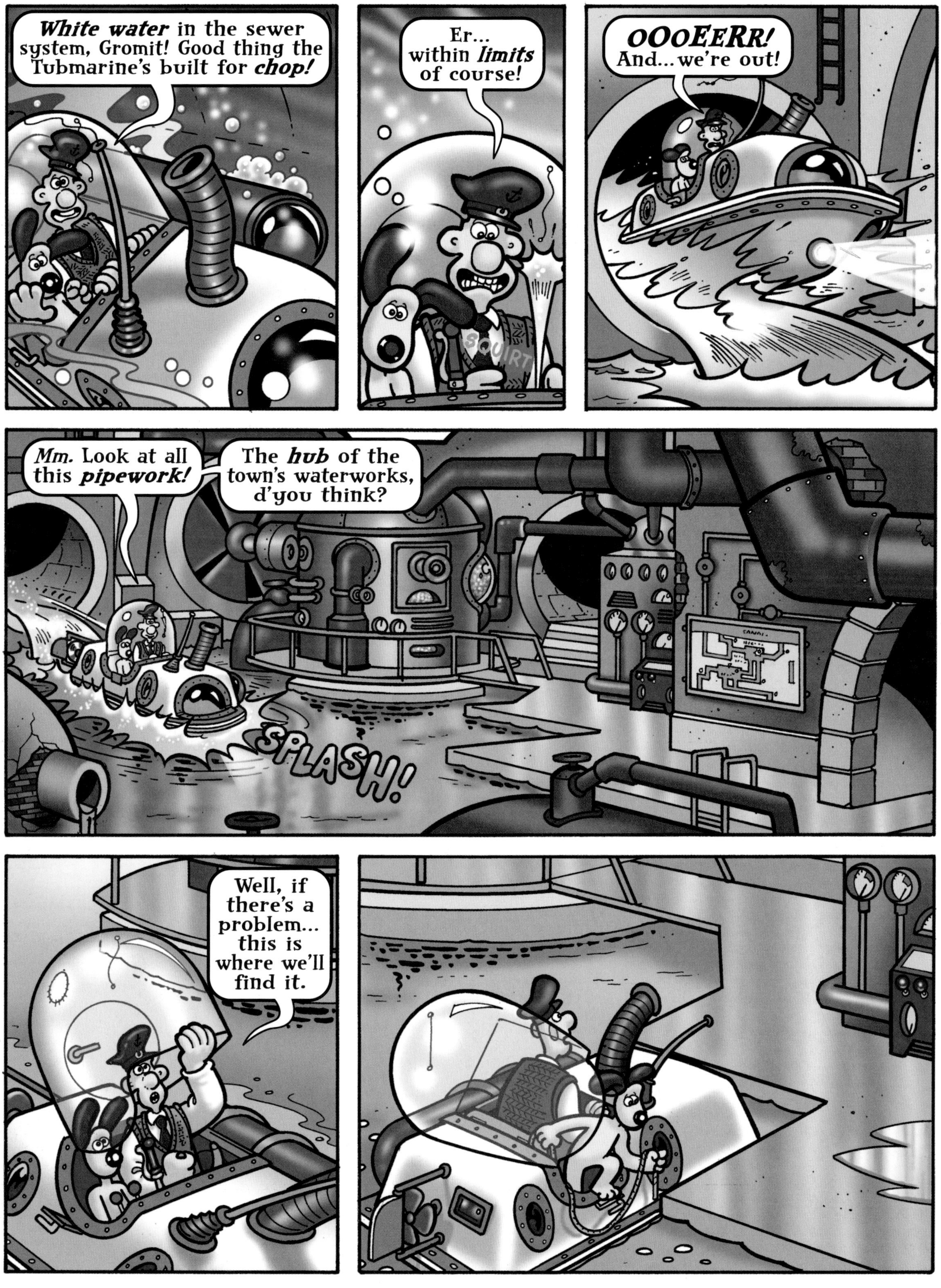
White water in the sewer system, Gromit! Good thing the Tubmarine's built for chop!
Er... within limits of course!
SQUIRT
OOOoEERR! And... we're out!
Mm. Look at all this pipework!
The hub of the town's waterworks, d'you think?
SPLASH!
Well, if there's a problem... this is where we'll find it.

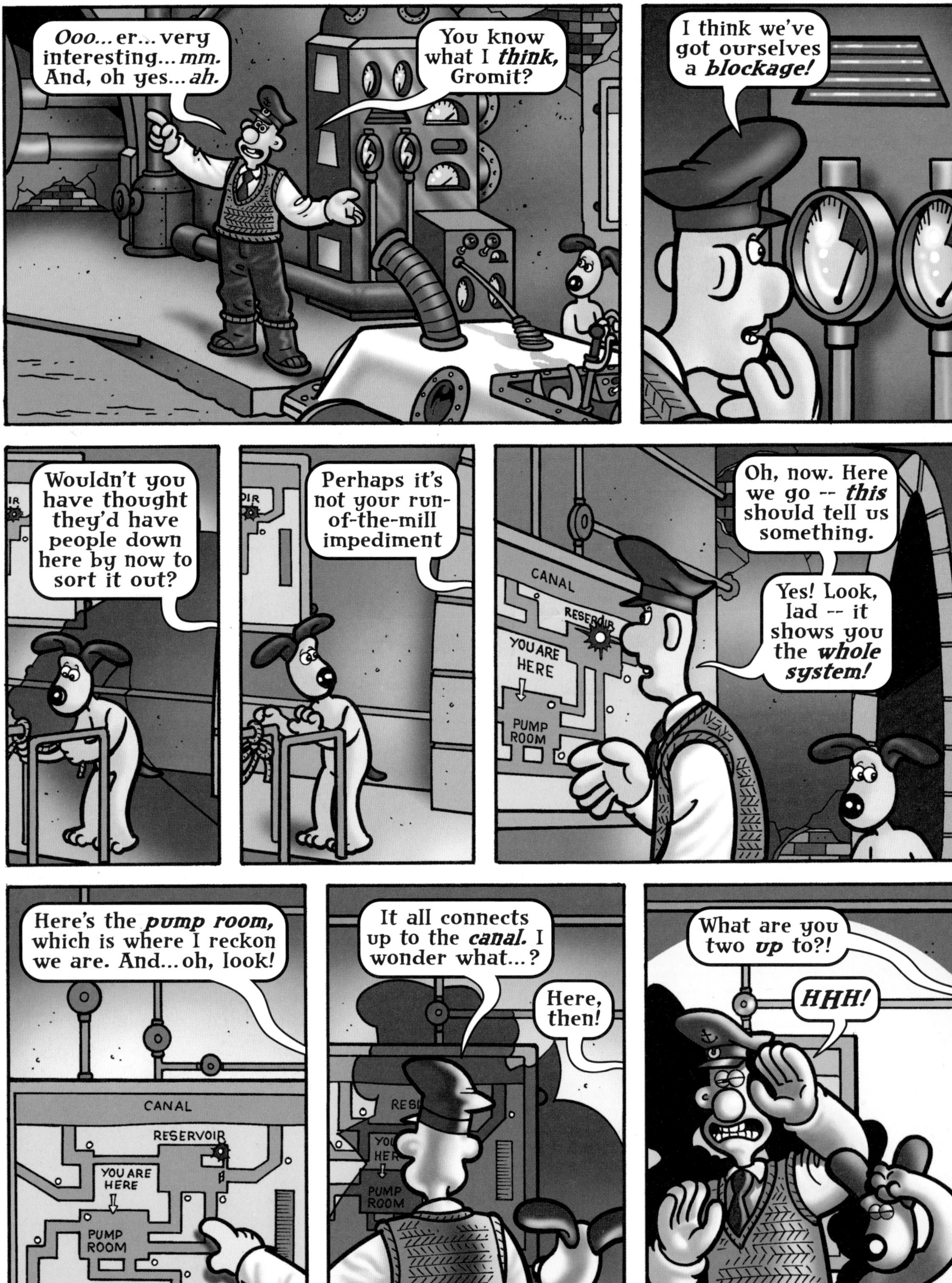

Ooo... er... very interesting... mm. And, oh yes... ah.
You know what I think, Gromit?
I think we've got ourselves a blockage!
Wouldn't you have thought they'd have people down here by now to sort it out?
Perhaps it's not your run-of-the-mill impediment
Oh, now. Here we go -- this should tell us something.
Yes! Look, lad -- it shows you the whole system!
CANAL
RESERVOIR
YOU ARE HERE
PUMP ROOM
Here's the pump room, which is where I reckon we are. And... oh, look!
CANAL
RESERVOIR
YOU ARE HERE
PUMP ROOM
It all connects up to the canal. I wonder what...?
Here, then!
What are you two up to?!
HHH!

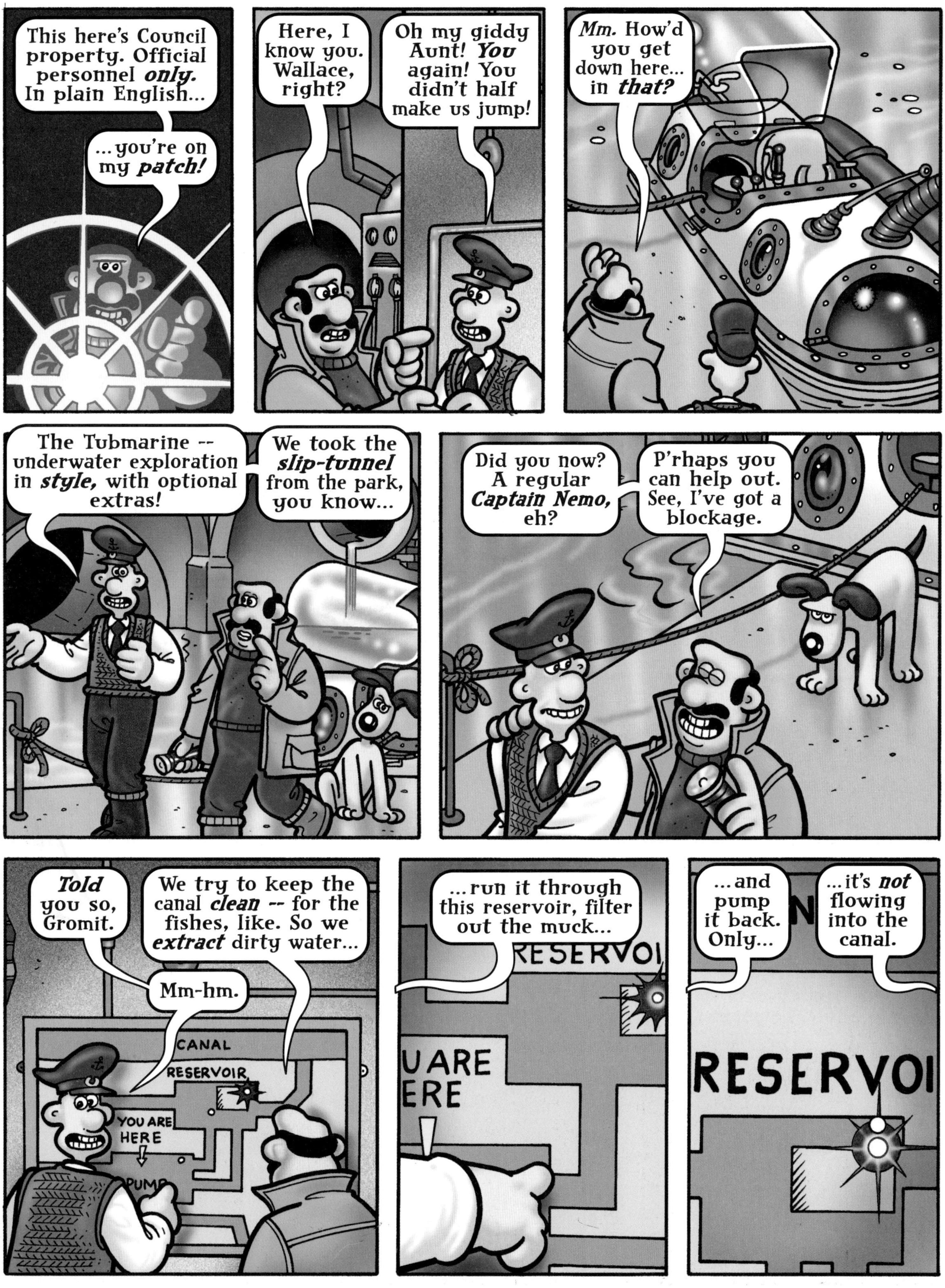
This here's Council property. Official personnel *only.* In plain English...
...you're on my *patch!*
Here, I know you. Wallace, right?
Oh my giddy Aunt! *You* again! You didn't half make us jump!
Mm. How'd you get down here... in *that?*
The Tubmarine -- underwater exploration in *style,* with optional extras!
We took the *slip-tunnel* from the park, you know...
Did you now? A regular *Captain Nemo,* eh?
P'rhaps you can help out. See, I've got a blockage.
Told you so, Gromit.
We try to keep the canal *clean* -- for the fishes, like. So we *extract* dirty water...
Mm-hm.
CANAL
RESERVOIR
YOU ARE HERE
...run it through this reservoir, filter out the muck...
RESERVOI
...and pump it back. Only...
...it's *not* flowing into the canal.
RESERVOI

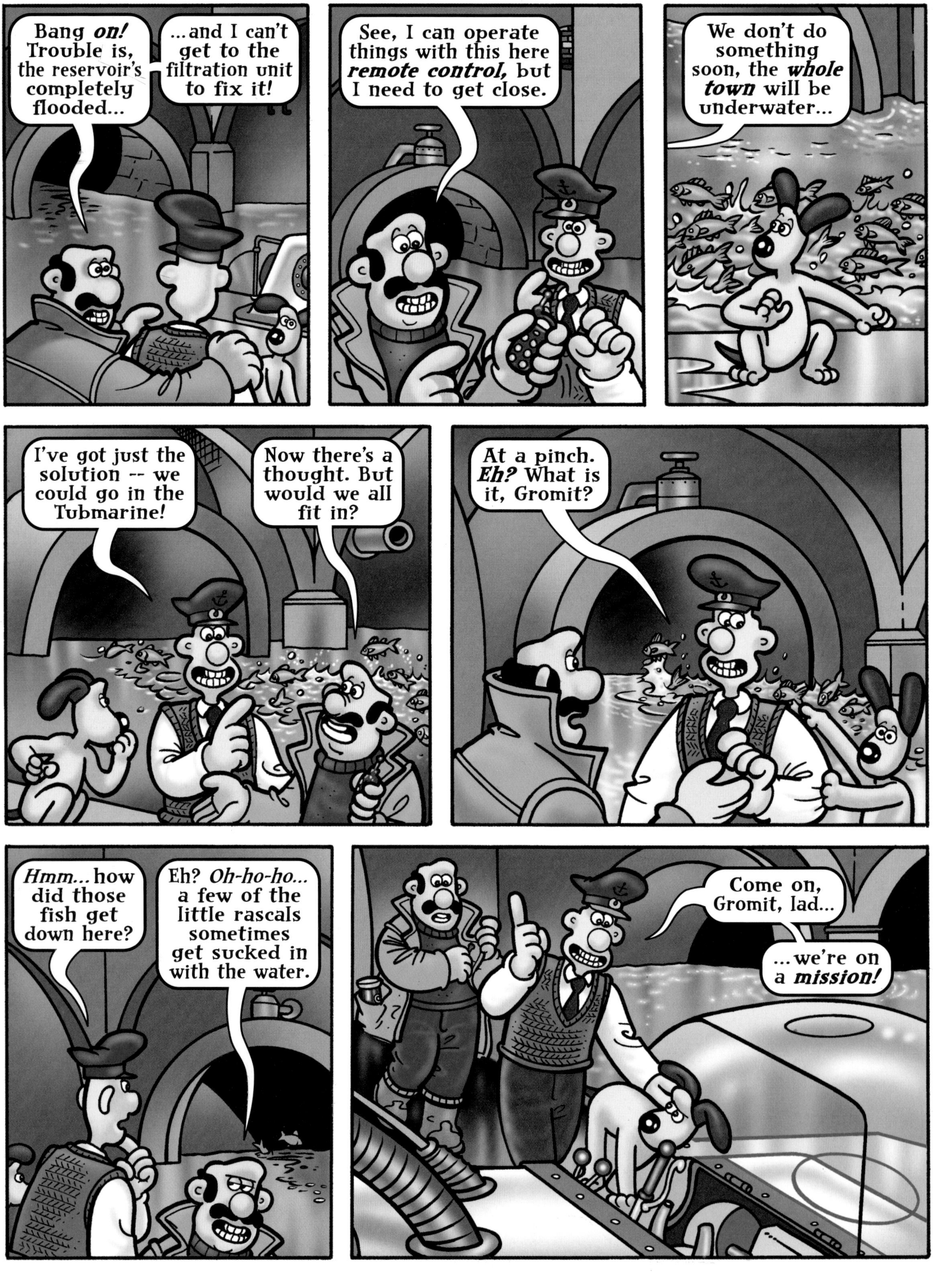
Bang on! Trouble is, the reservoir's completely flooded...
...and I can't get to the filtration unit to fix it!
See, I can operate things with this here remote control, but I need to get close.
We don't do something soon, the whole town will be underwater...
I've got just the solution -- we could go in the Tubmarine!
Now there's a thought. But would we all fit in?
At a pinch. Eh? What is it, Gromit?
Hmm... how did those fish get down here?
Eh? Oh-ho-ho... a few of the little rascals sometimes get sucked in with the water.
Come on, Gromit, lad...
...we're on a mission!

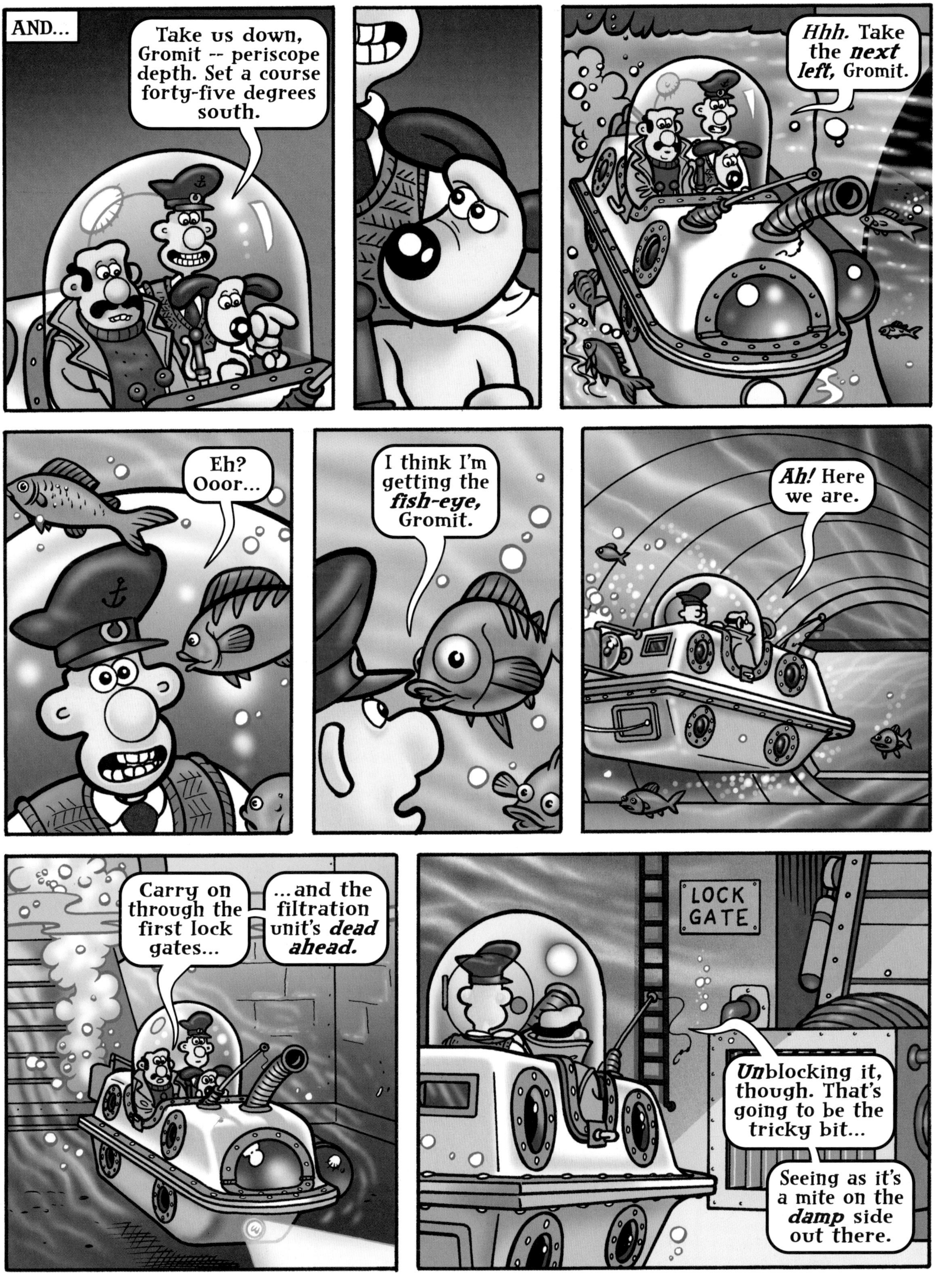
AND...
Take us down, Gromit -- periscope depth. Set a course forty-five degrees south.
Hhh. Take the ***next left,*** Gromit.
Eh? Ooor...
I think I'm getting the ***fish-eye,*** Gromit.
Ah! Here we are.
Carry on through the first lock gates...
...and the filtration unit's ***dead ahead.***
LOCK GATE
Unblocking it, though. That's going to be the tricky bit...
Seeing as it's a mite on the ***damp*** side out there.

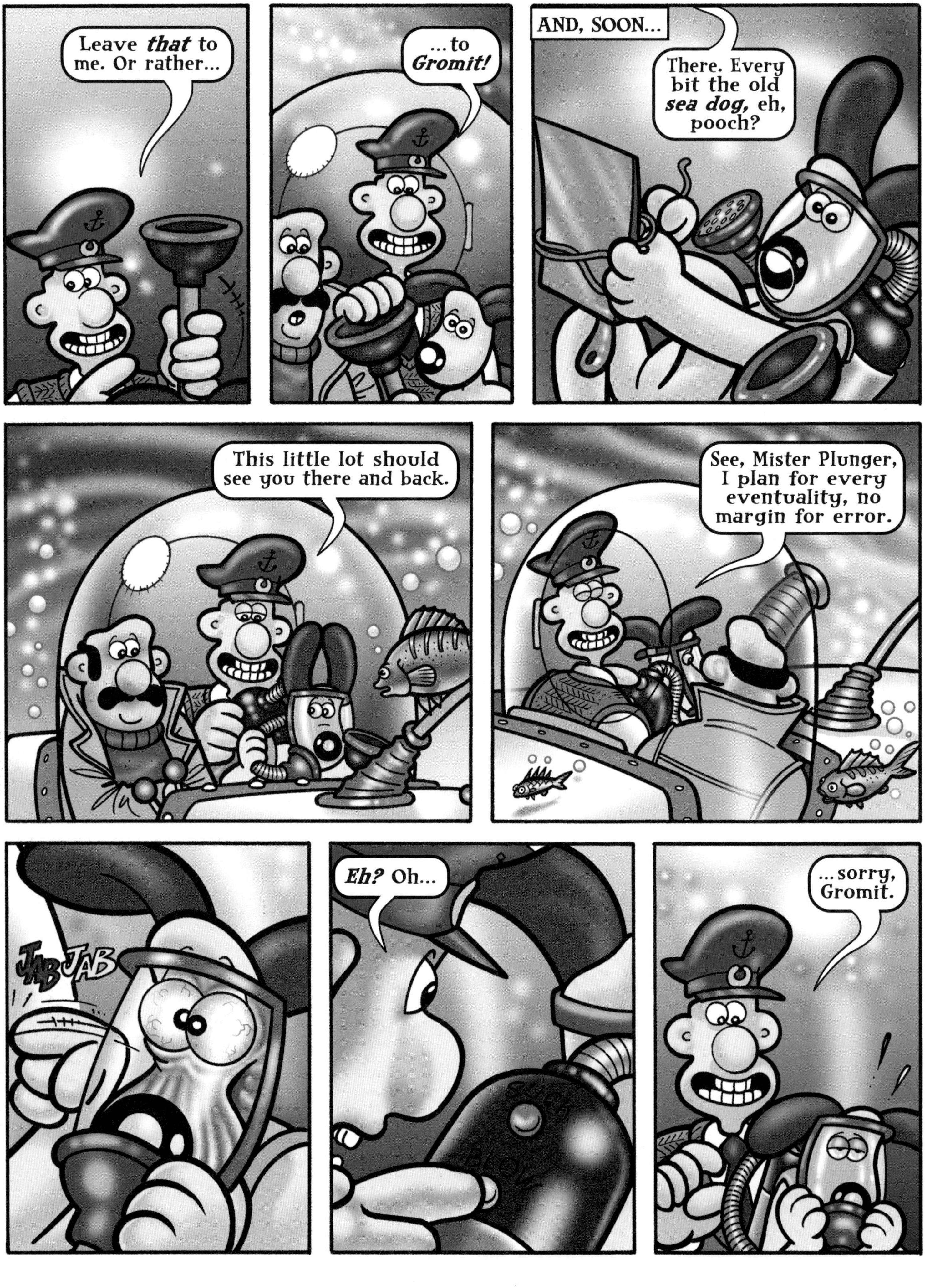
Leave *that* to me. Or rather...
...to *Gromit!*
AND, SOON...
There. Every bit the old *sea dog,* eh, pooch?
This little lot should see you there and back.
See, Mister Plunger, I plan for every eventuality, no margin for error.
JAB JAB
Eh? Oh...
SUCK
BLOW
...sorry, Gromit.

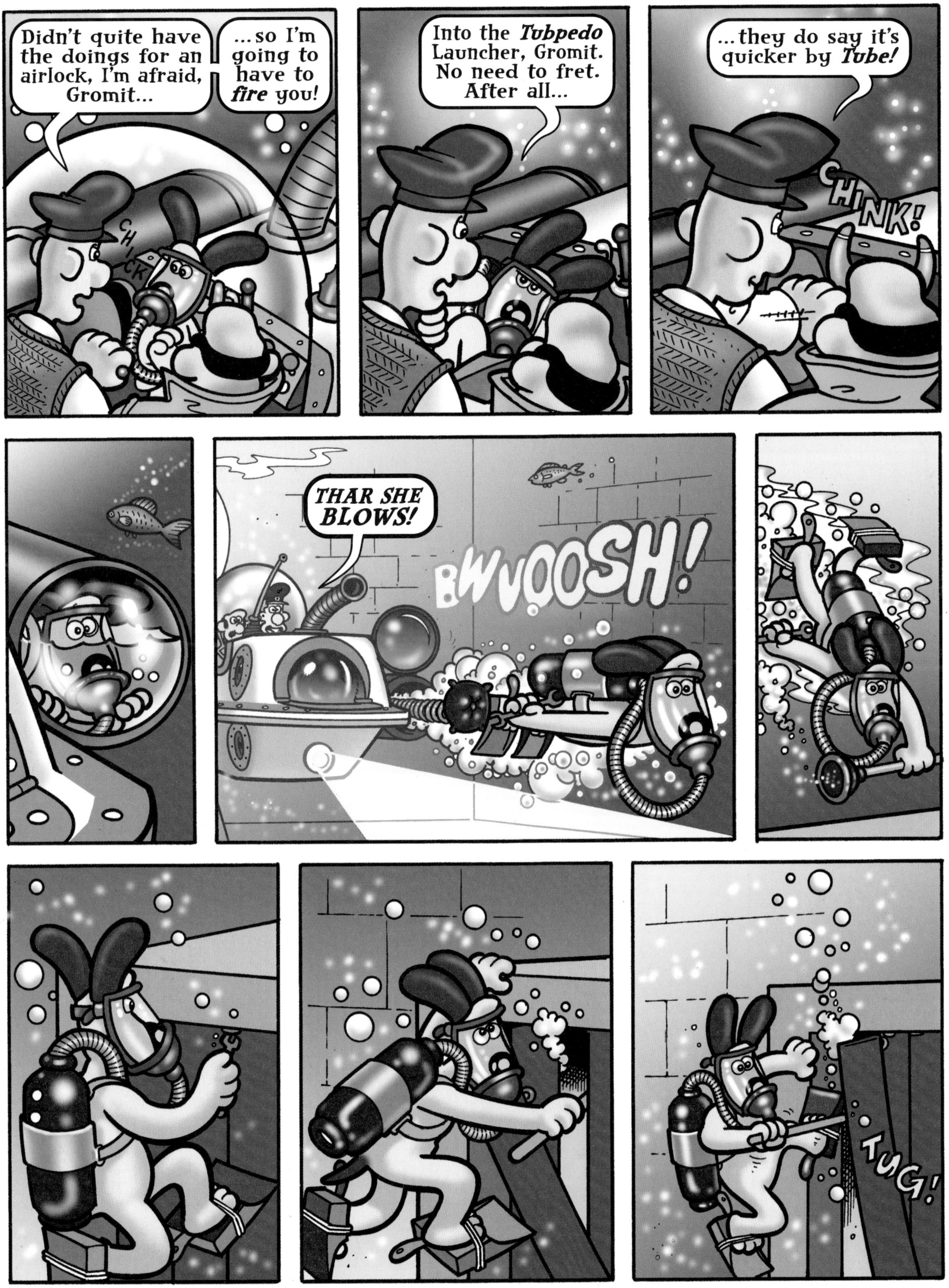
Didn't quite have the doings for an airlock, I'm afraid, Gromit...
...so I'm going to have to *fire* you!
CHICK
Into the *Tubpedo* Launcher, Gromit. No need to fret. After all...
...they do say it's quicker by *Tube!*
CHINK!
THAR SHE BLOWS!
BWVOOSH!
TUG!

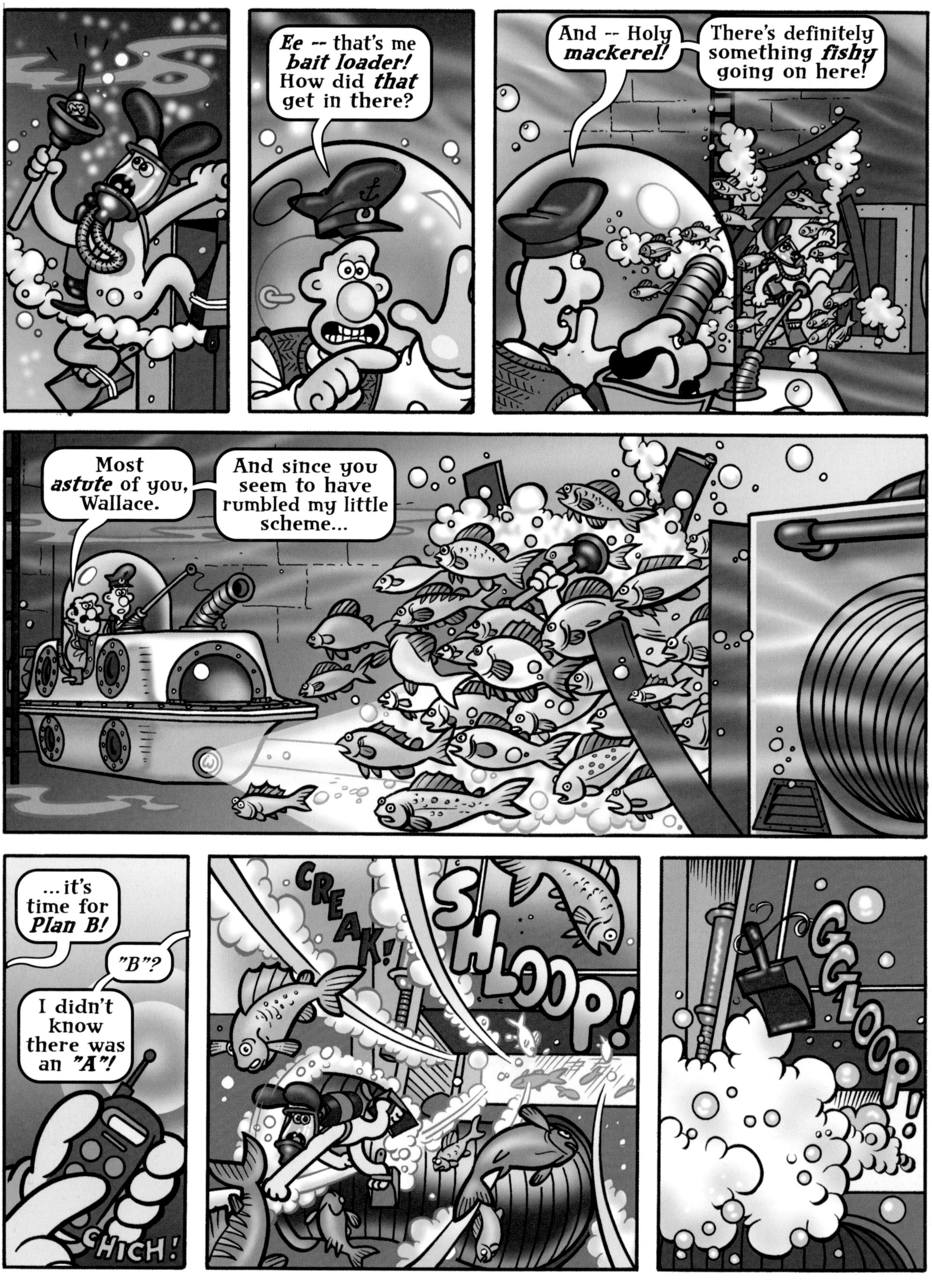
Ee -- that's me bait loader! How did that get in there?
And -- Holy mackerel!
There's definitely something fishy going on here!
Most astute of you, Wallace.
And since you seem to have rumbled my little scheme...
...it's time for Plan B!
"B"?
I didn't know there was an "A"!
CHICH!
CREAK!
SHLOOP!
GGLOOP!

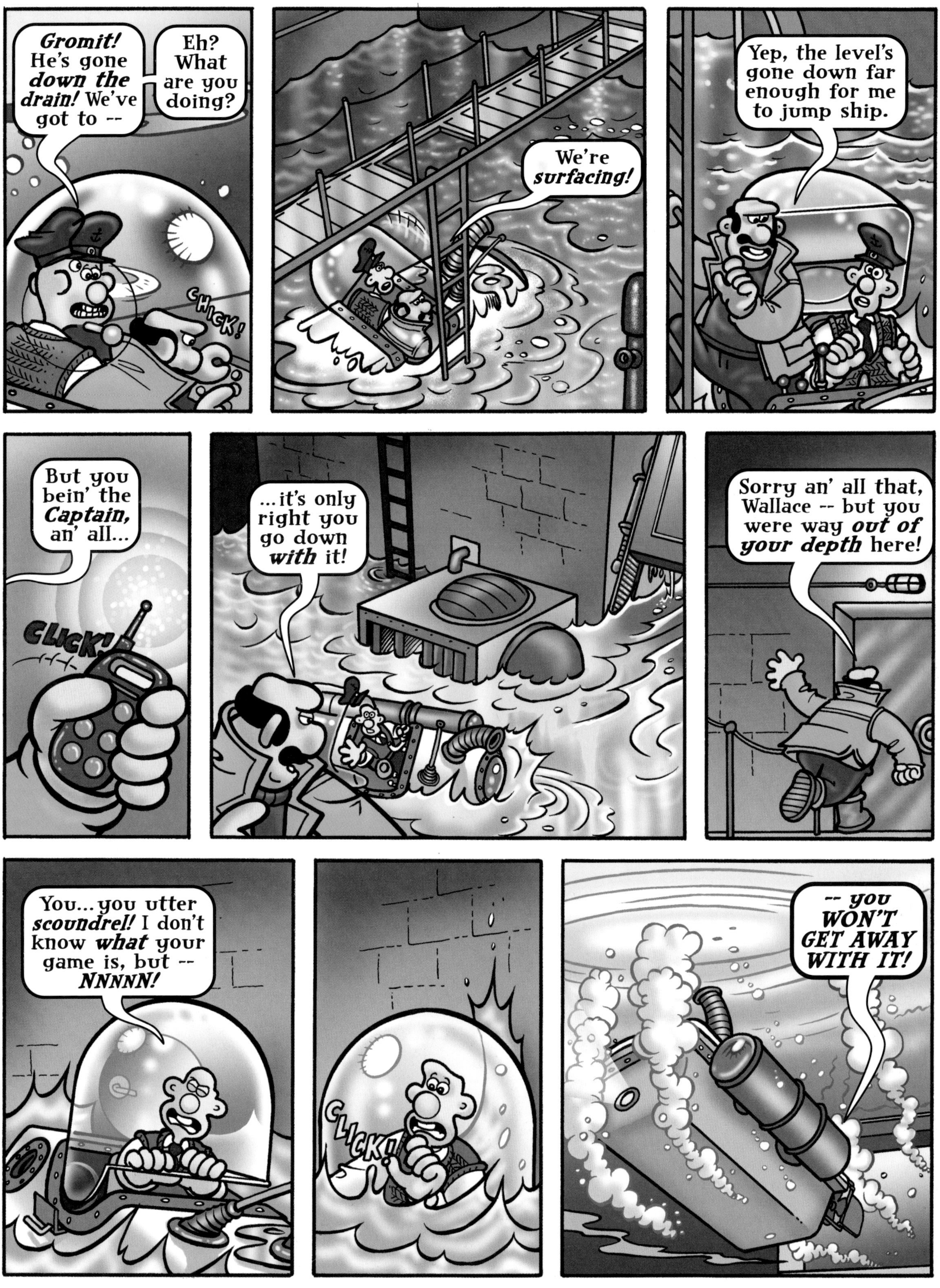
Gromit! He's gone down the drain! We've got to --
Eh? What are you doing?
CHICK!
We're surfacing!
Yep, the level's gone down far enough for me to jump ship.
But you bein' the Captain, an' all...
CLICK!
...it's only right you go down with it!
Sorry an' all that, Wallace -- but you were way out of your depth here!
You... you utter scoundrel! I don't know what your game is, but -- NNNNN!
CLICK!
-- you WON'T GET AWAY WITH IT!

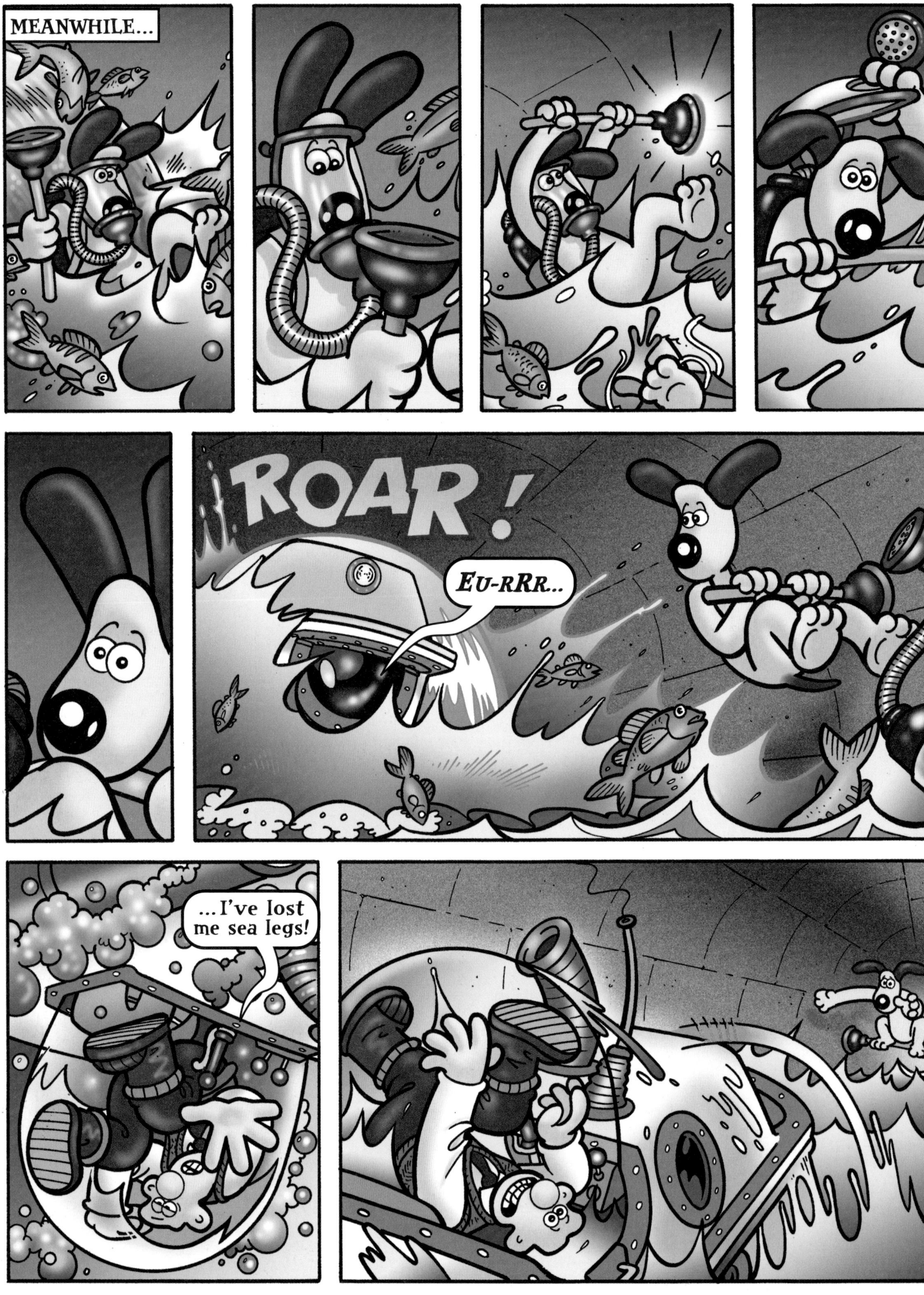
MEANWHILE...
¡ROAR!
EU-RRR...
...I've lost me sea legs!

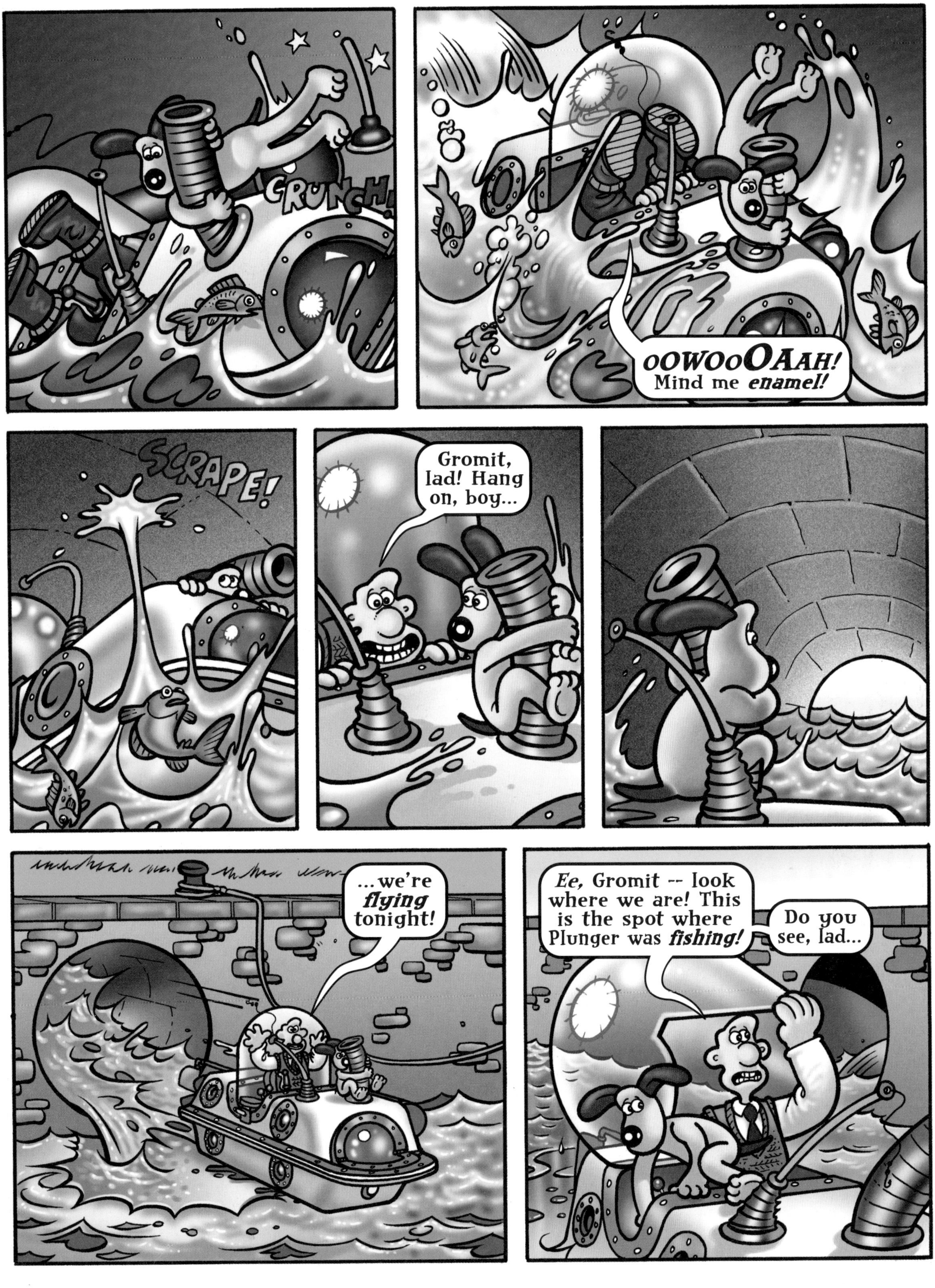
CRUNCH!
OOWOoOAAH! Mind me enamel!
SCRAPE!
Gromit, lad! Hang on, boy...
...we're flying tonight!
Ee, Gromit -- look where we are! This is the spot where Plunger was fishing!
Do you see, lad...

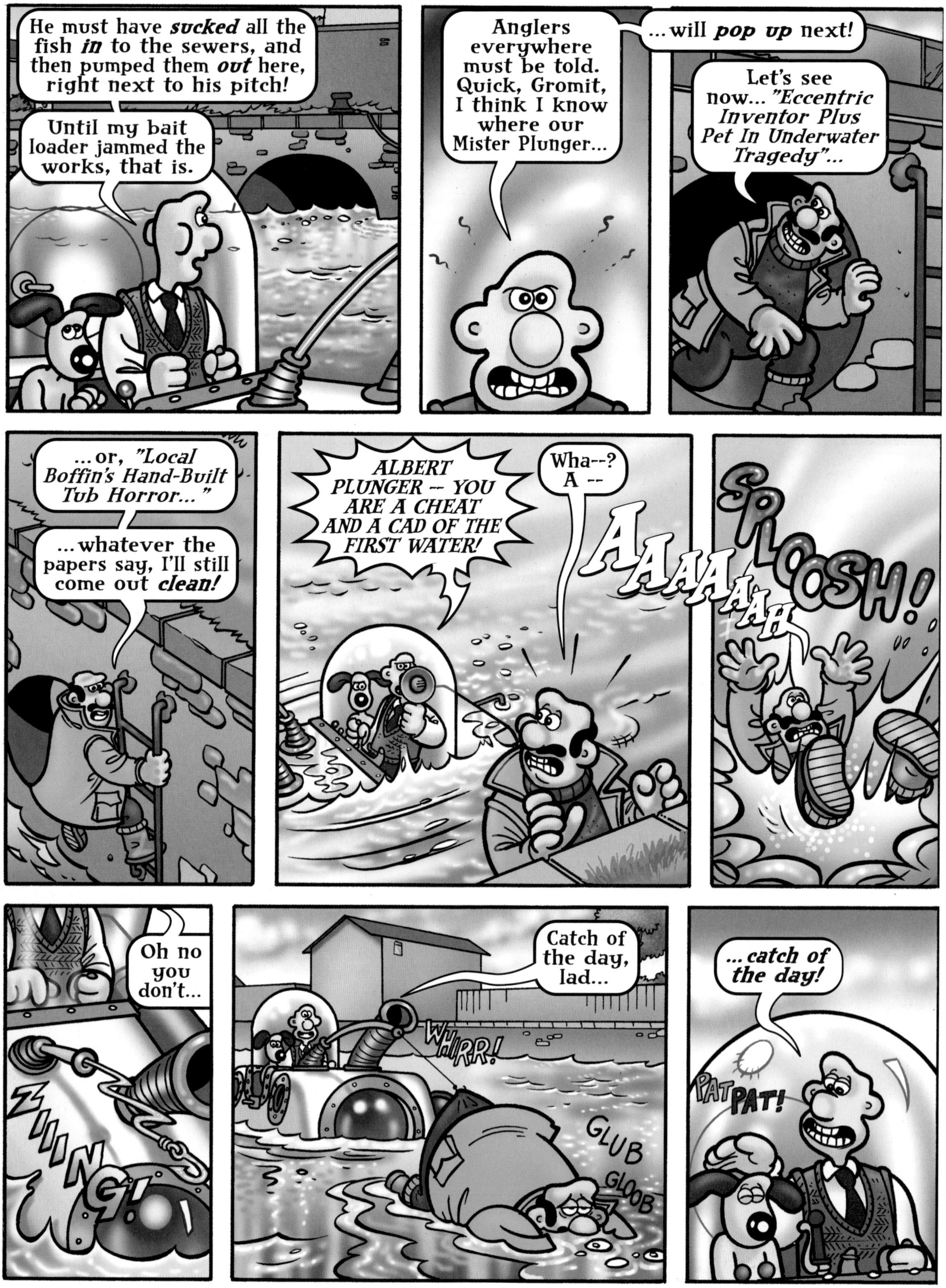

He must have *sucked* all the fish *in* to the sewers, and then pumped them *out* here, right next to his pitch!
Until my bait loader jammed the works, that is.
Anglers everywhere must be told. Quick, Gromit, I think I know where our Mister Plunger...
...will *pop up* next!
Let's see now... *"Eccentric Inventor Plus Pet In Underwater Tragedy"*...
...or, *"Local Boffin's Hand-Built Tub Horror..."*
...whatever the papers say, I'll still come out *clean!*
ALBERT PLUNGER -- YOU ARE A CHEAT AND A CAD OF THE FIRST WATER!
Wha--? A --
AAAAAAH
SPLOOSH!
Oh no you don't...
ZIIING!
Catch of the day, lad...
WHIRR!
GLUB
GLOOB
...catch of the day!
PAT PAT!

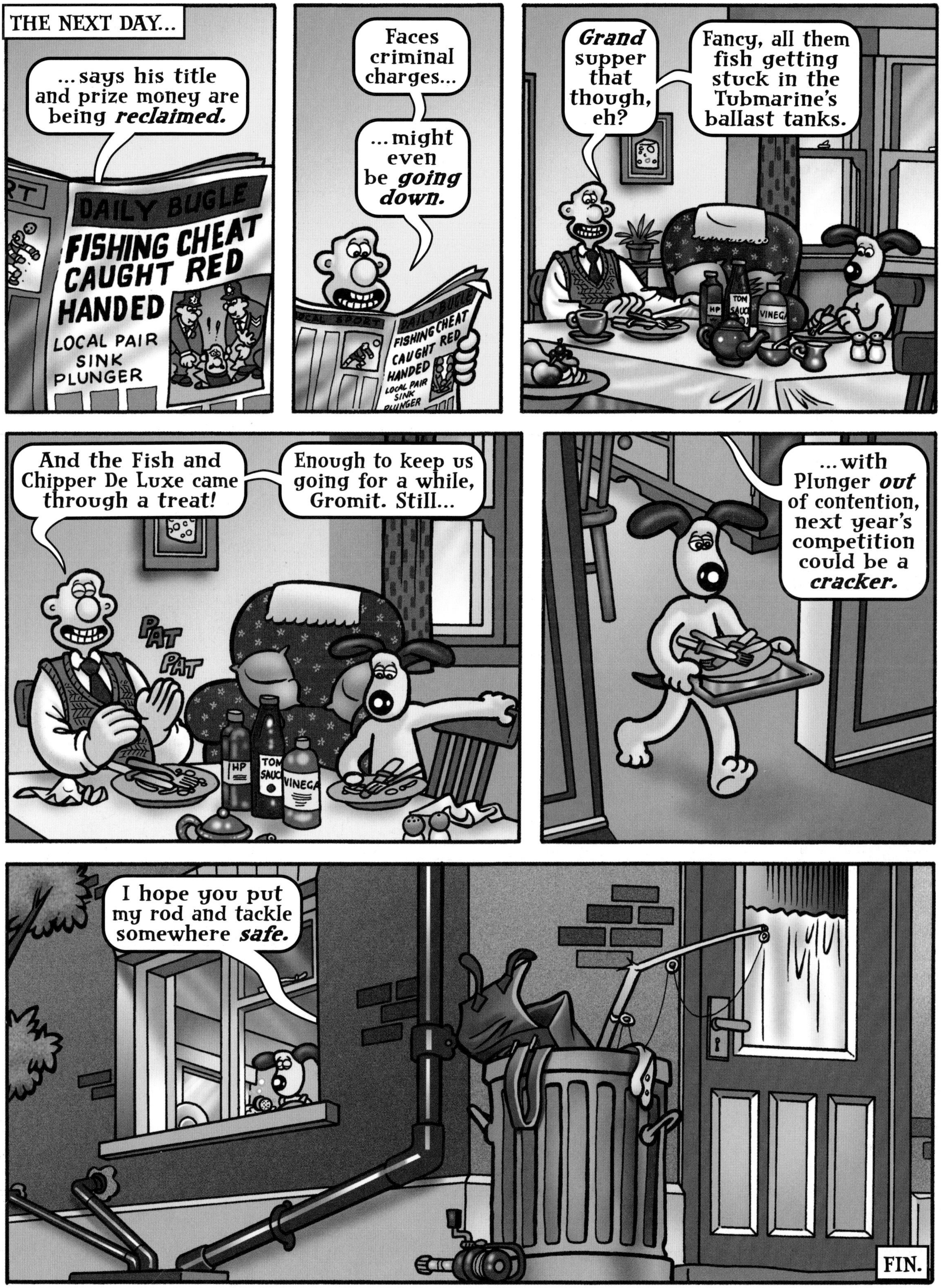
THE NEXT DAY...
...says his title and prize money are being *reclaimed.*
DAILY BUGLE
FISHING CHEAT CAUGHT RED HANDED
LOCAL PAIR SINK PLUNGER
Faces criminal charges...
...might even be *going down.*
Grand supper that though, eh?
Fancy, all them fish getting stuck in the Tubmarine's ballast tanks.
And the Fish and Chipper De Luxe came through a treat!
PAT PAT
Enough to keep us going for a while, Gromit. Still...
...with Plunger *out* of contention, next year's competition could be a *cracker.*
I hope you put my rod and tackle somewhere *safe.*
FIN.

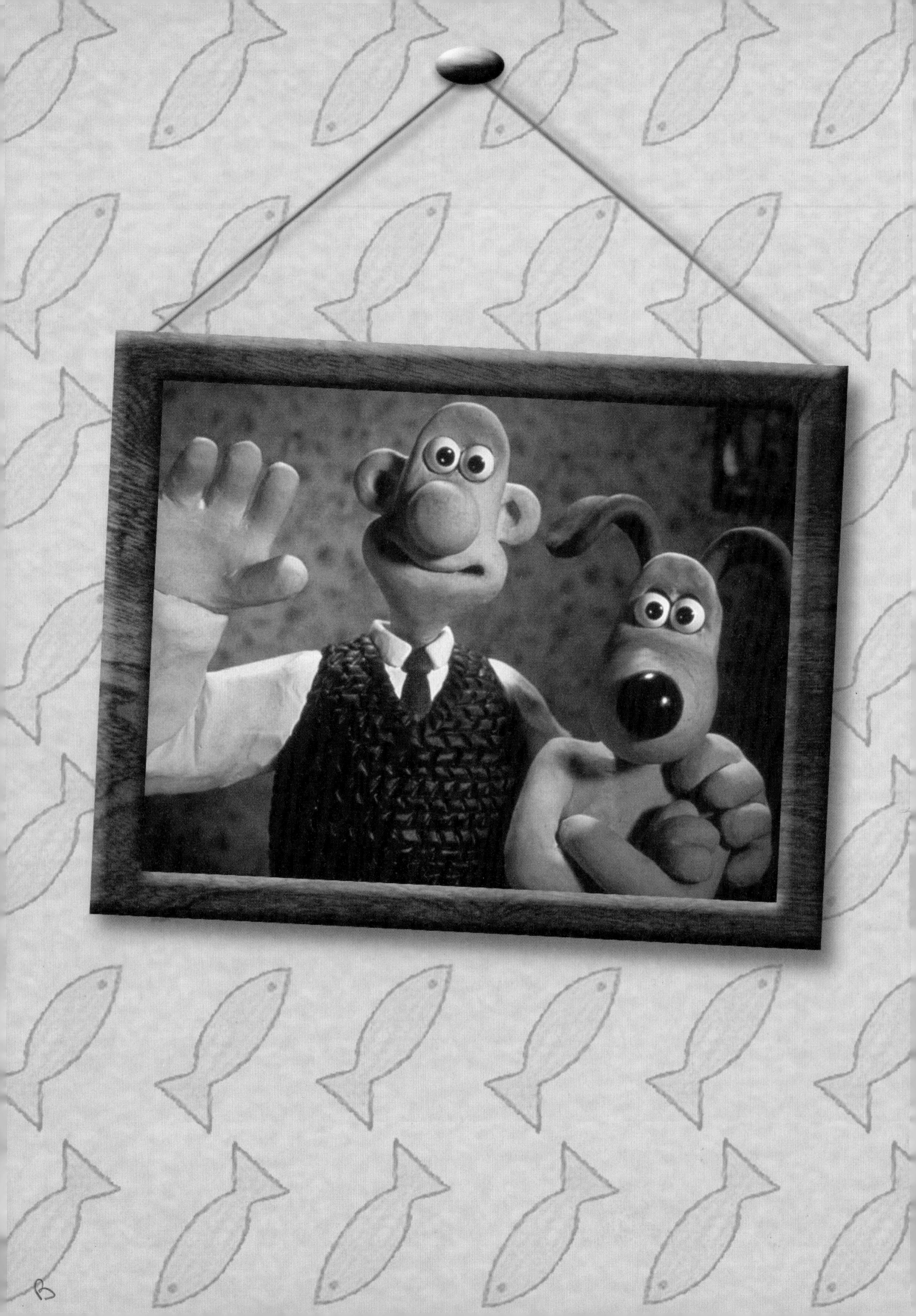

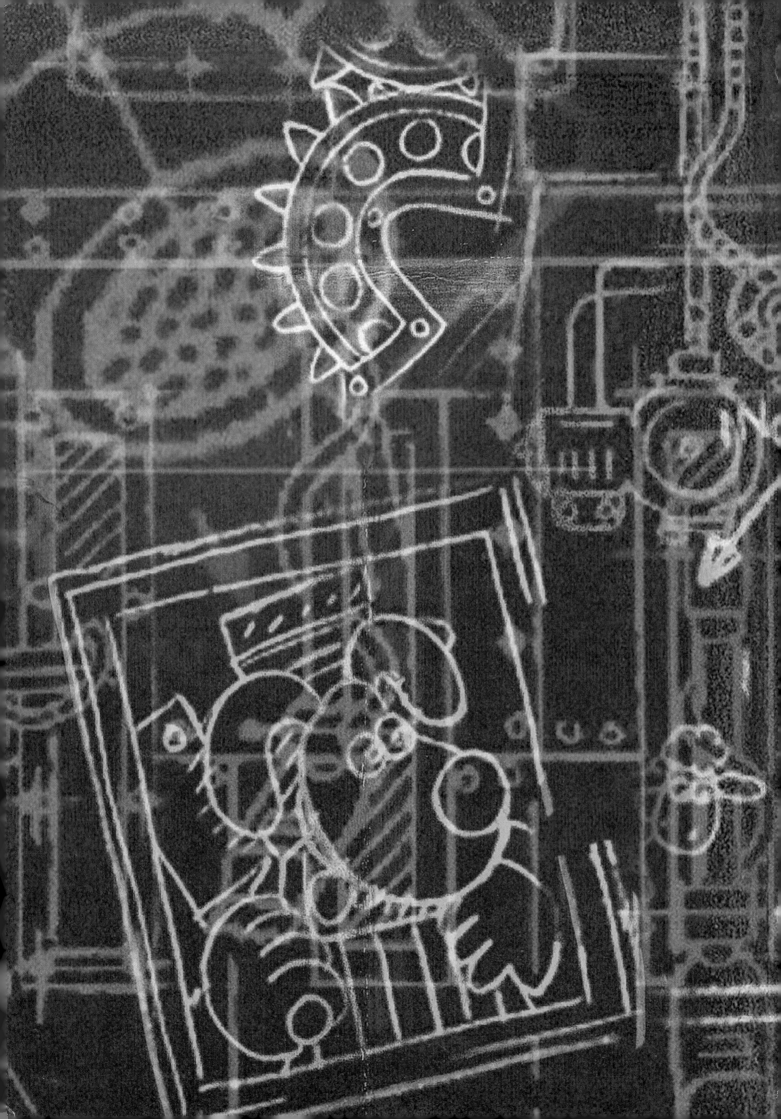